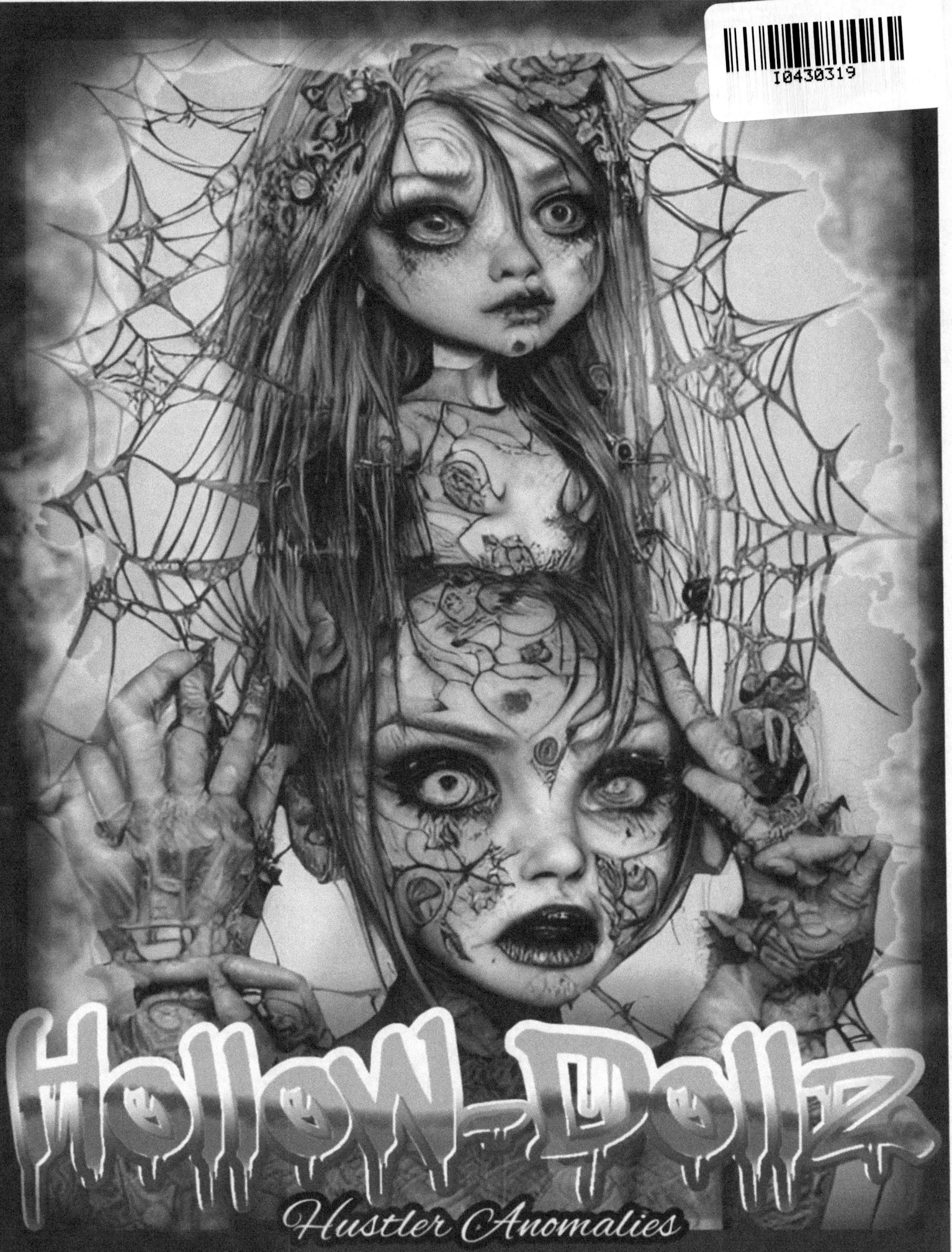

THIS BOOK IS DEDICATED TO THOSE THAT ALWAYS BELIEVED IN ME WITH A SPECIAL THANKS TO MY MOST BEAUTIFUL MOTHER

Copyright 2022 Deserius Arte

All rights reserved. This book or any portion thereof may not be reproduced nor used in any matter whatsoever without the express written permission of the publisher except for the use of brief quotations in a book review.

Printed by HUSTLER ANOMALIES in the USA

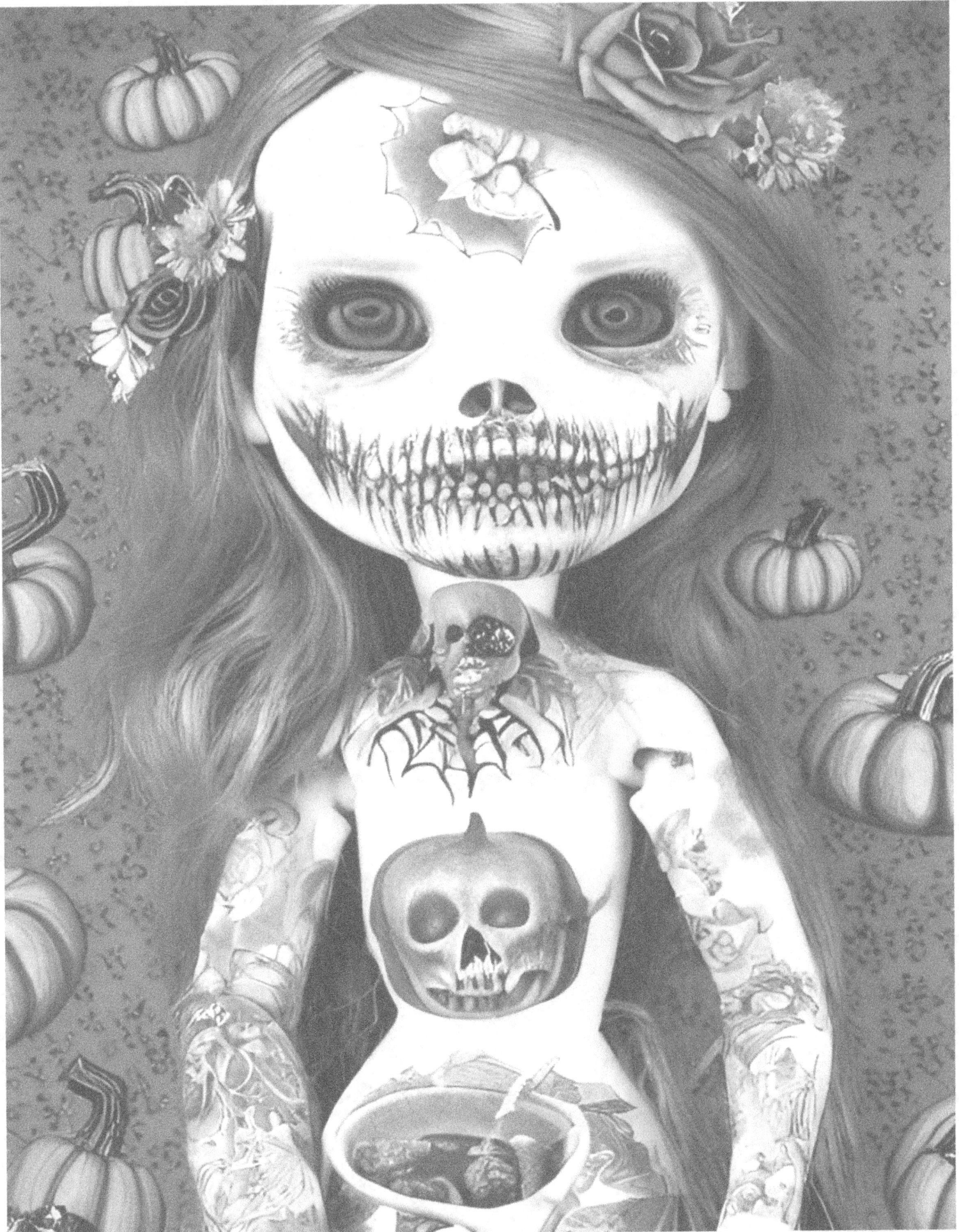

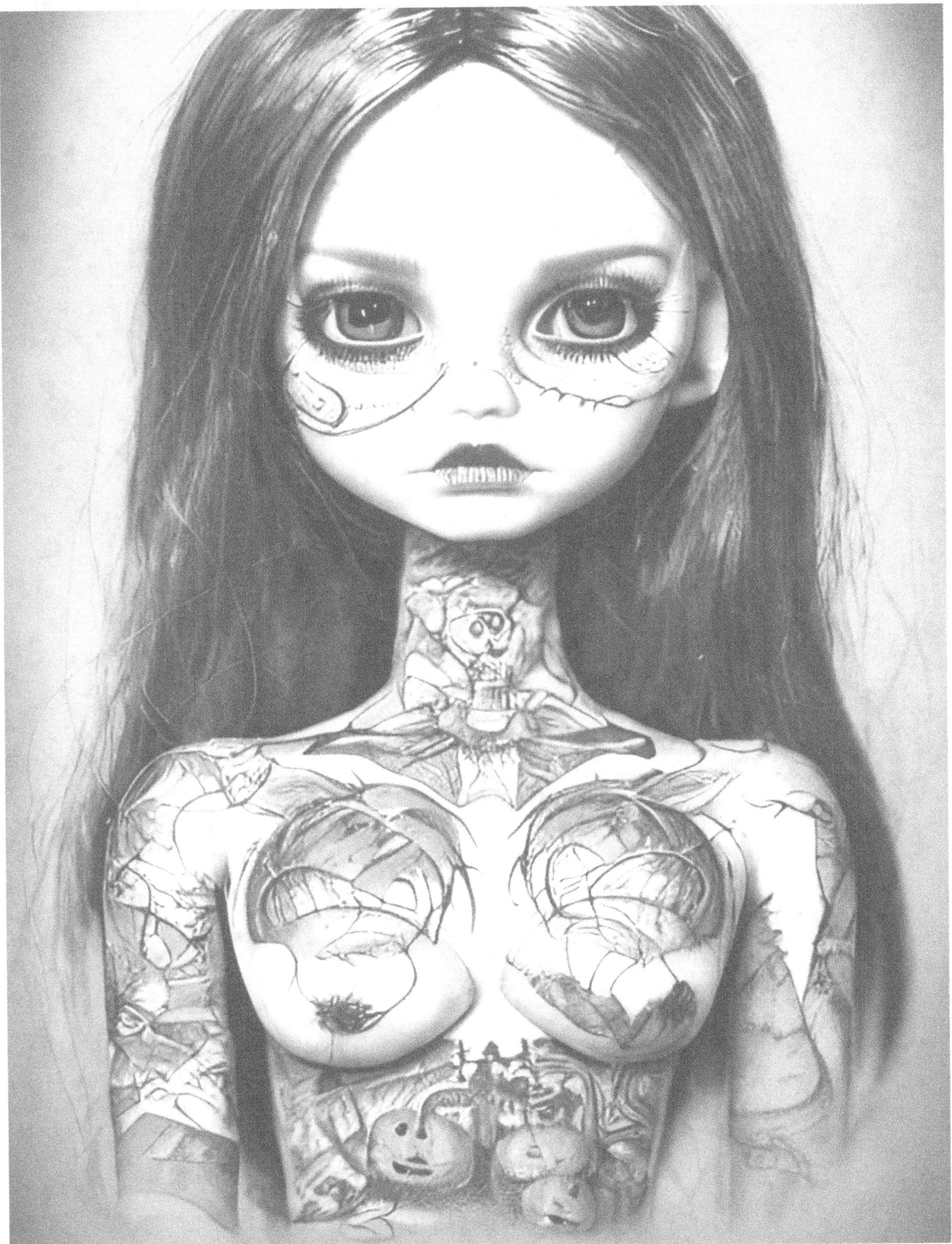

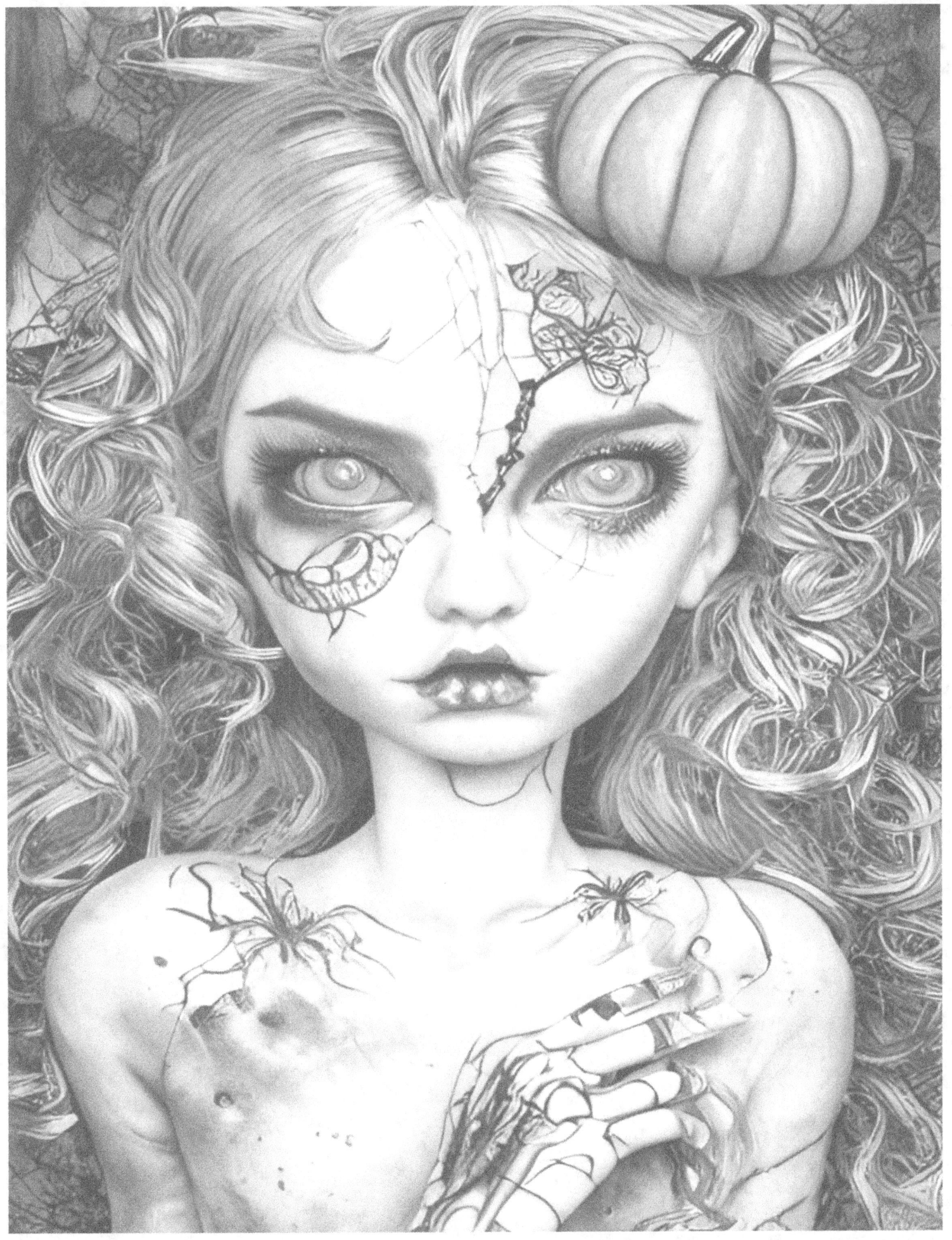

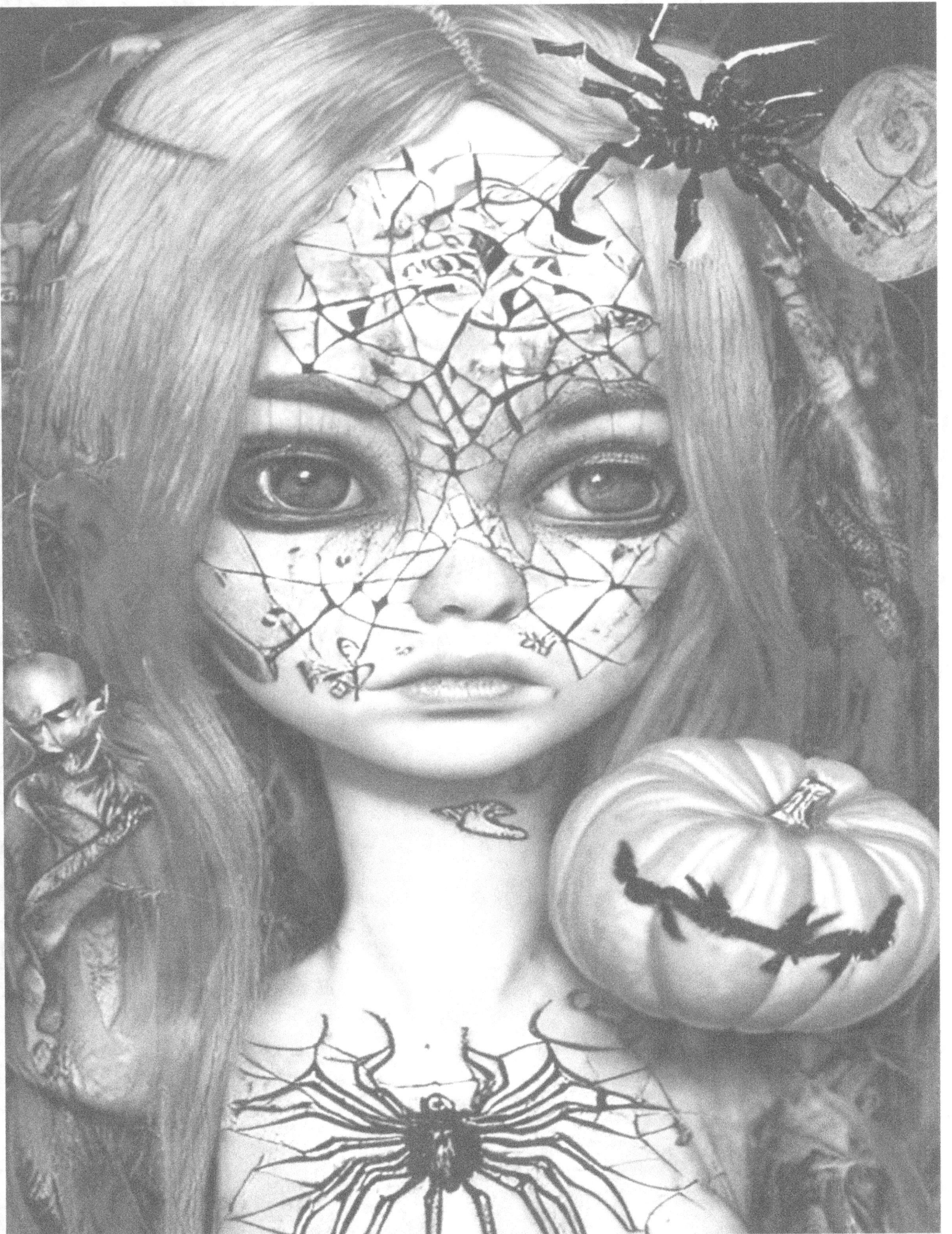

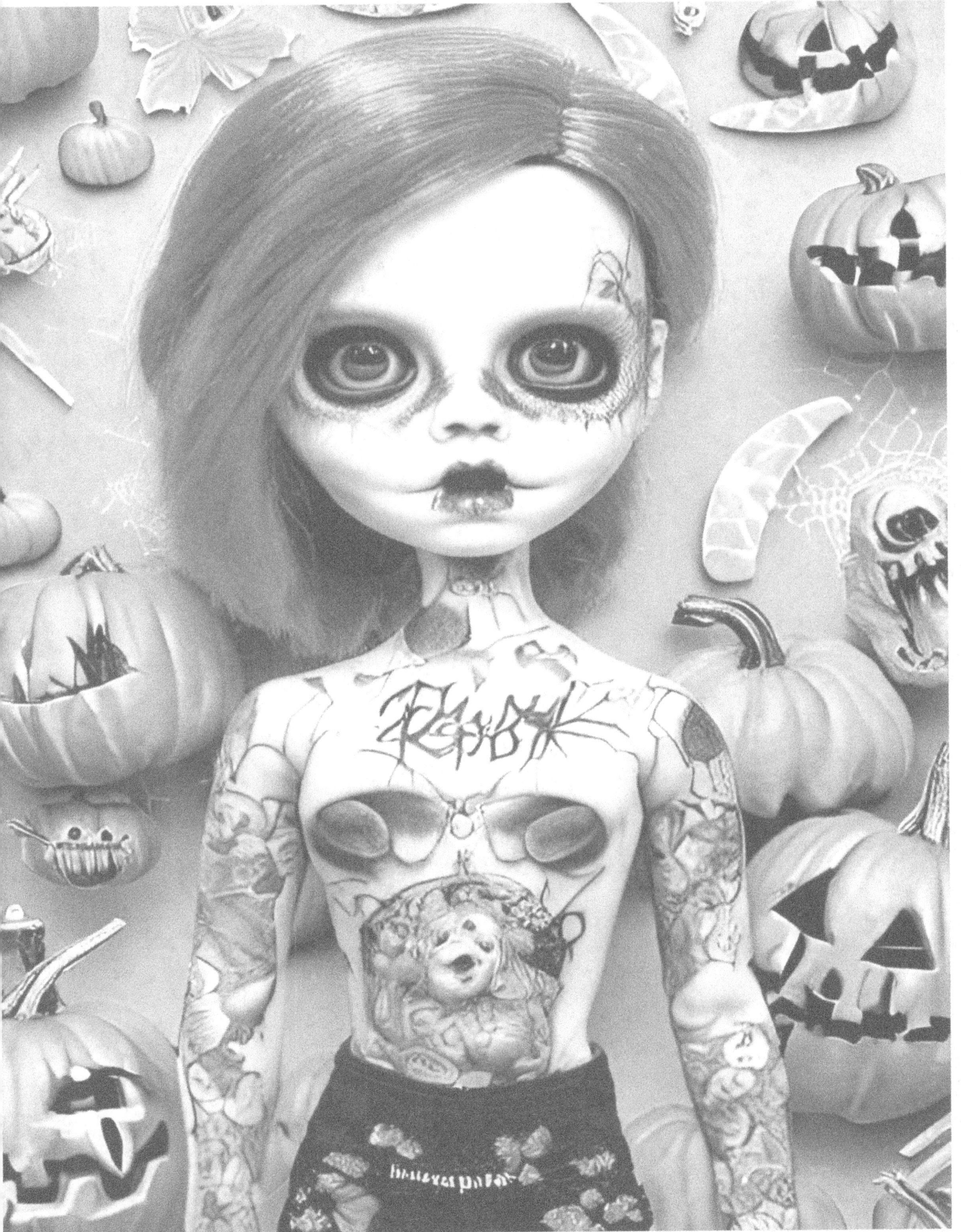

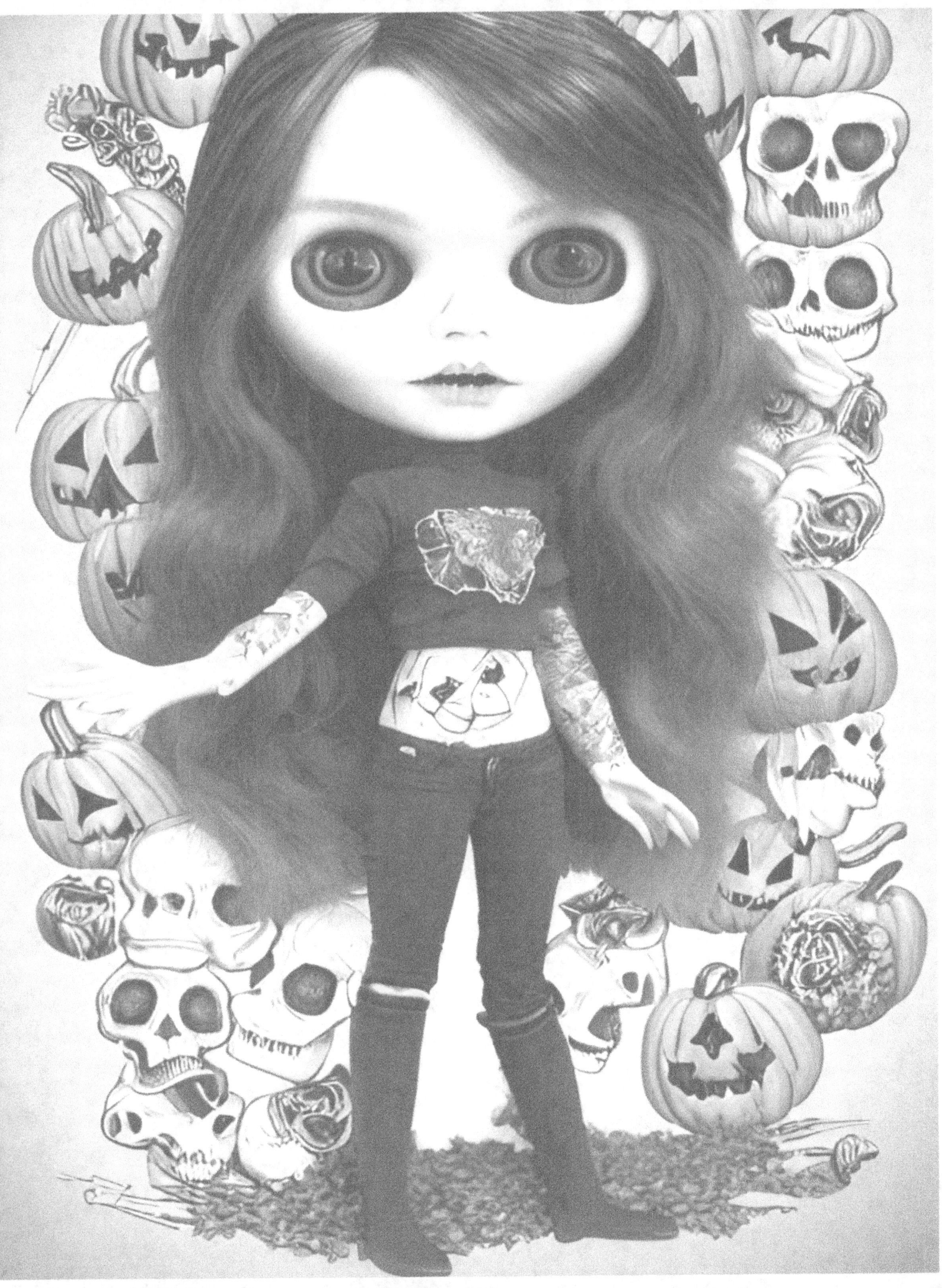

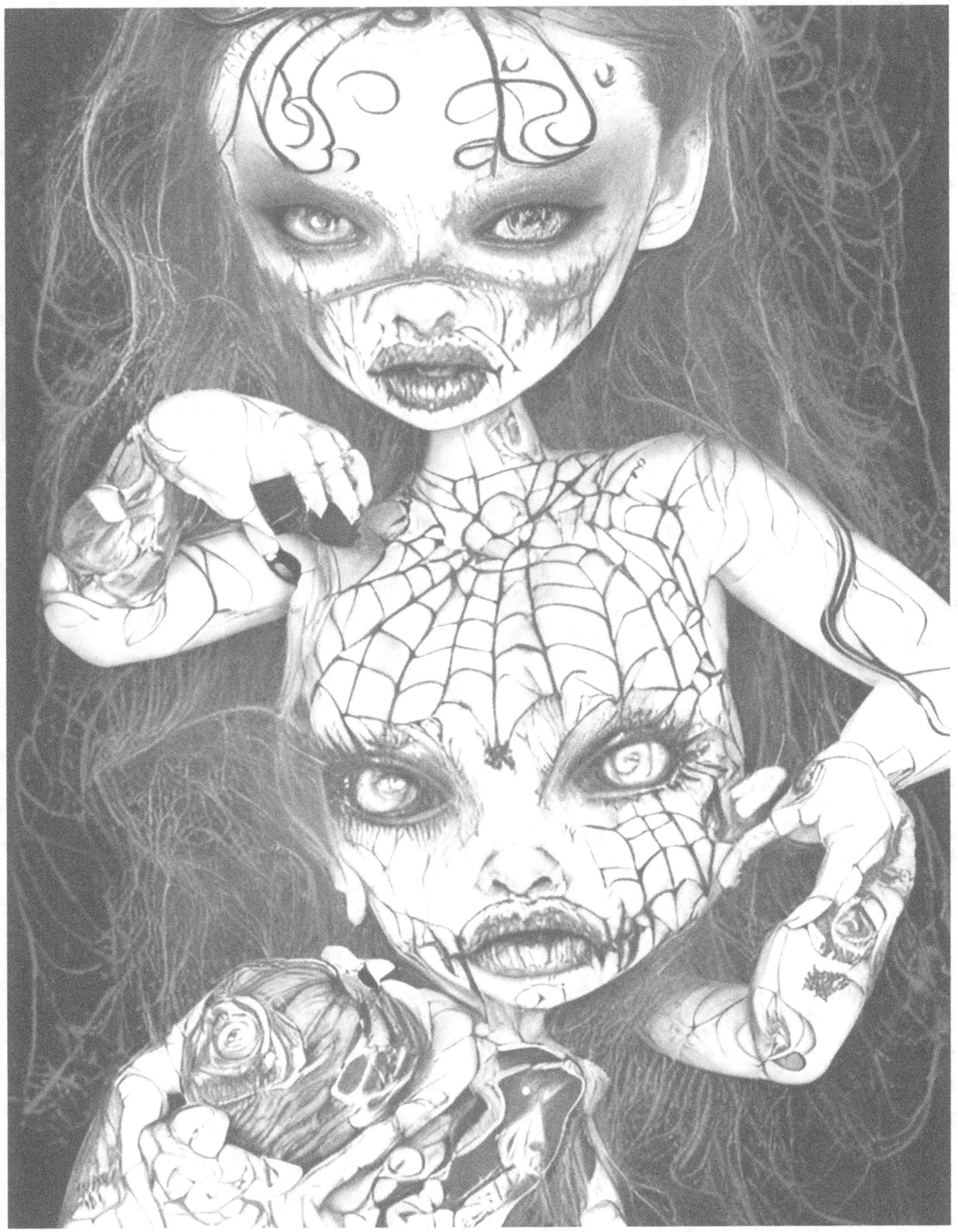

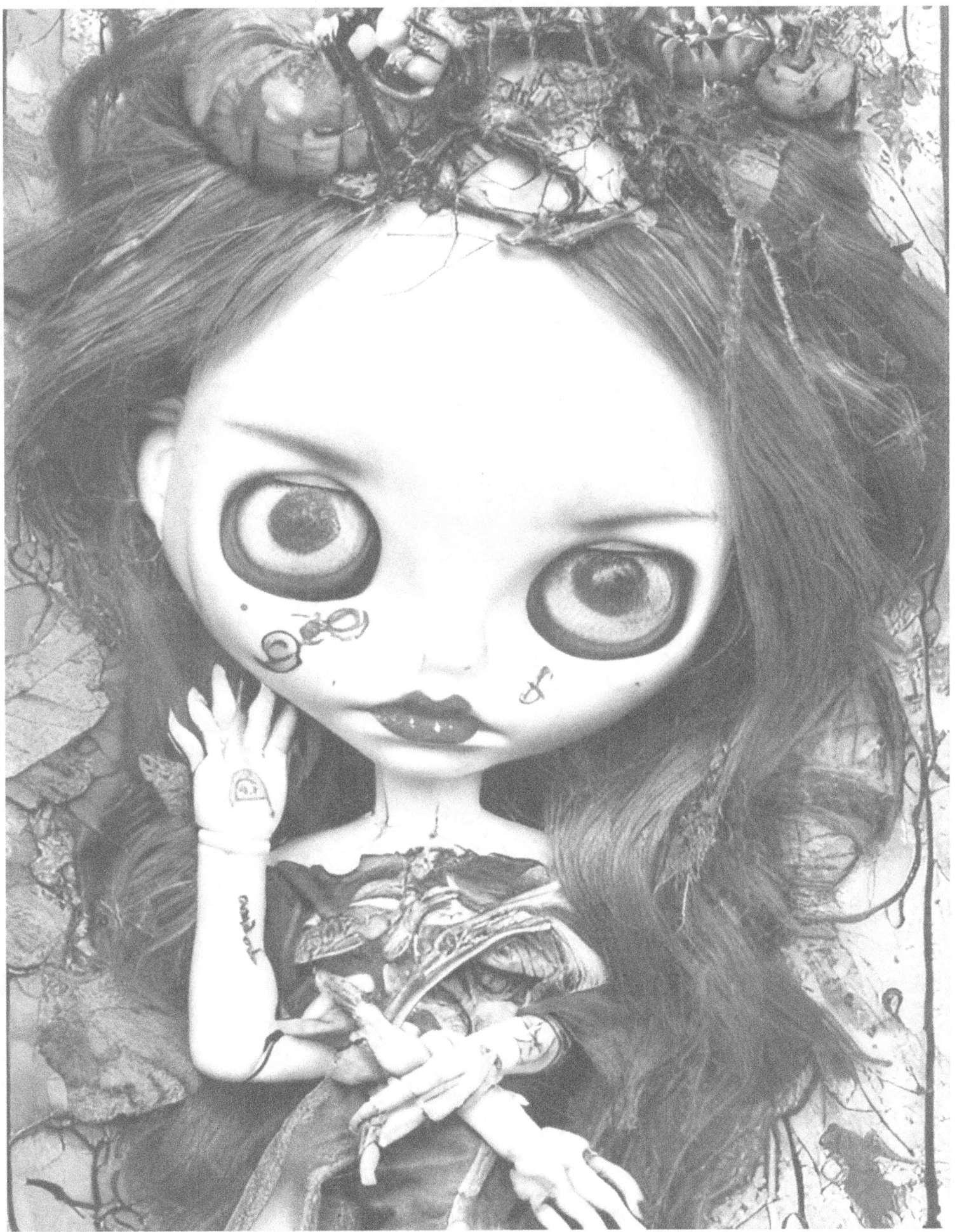

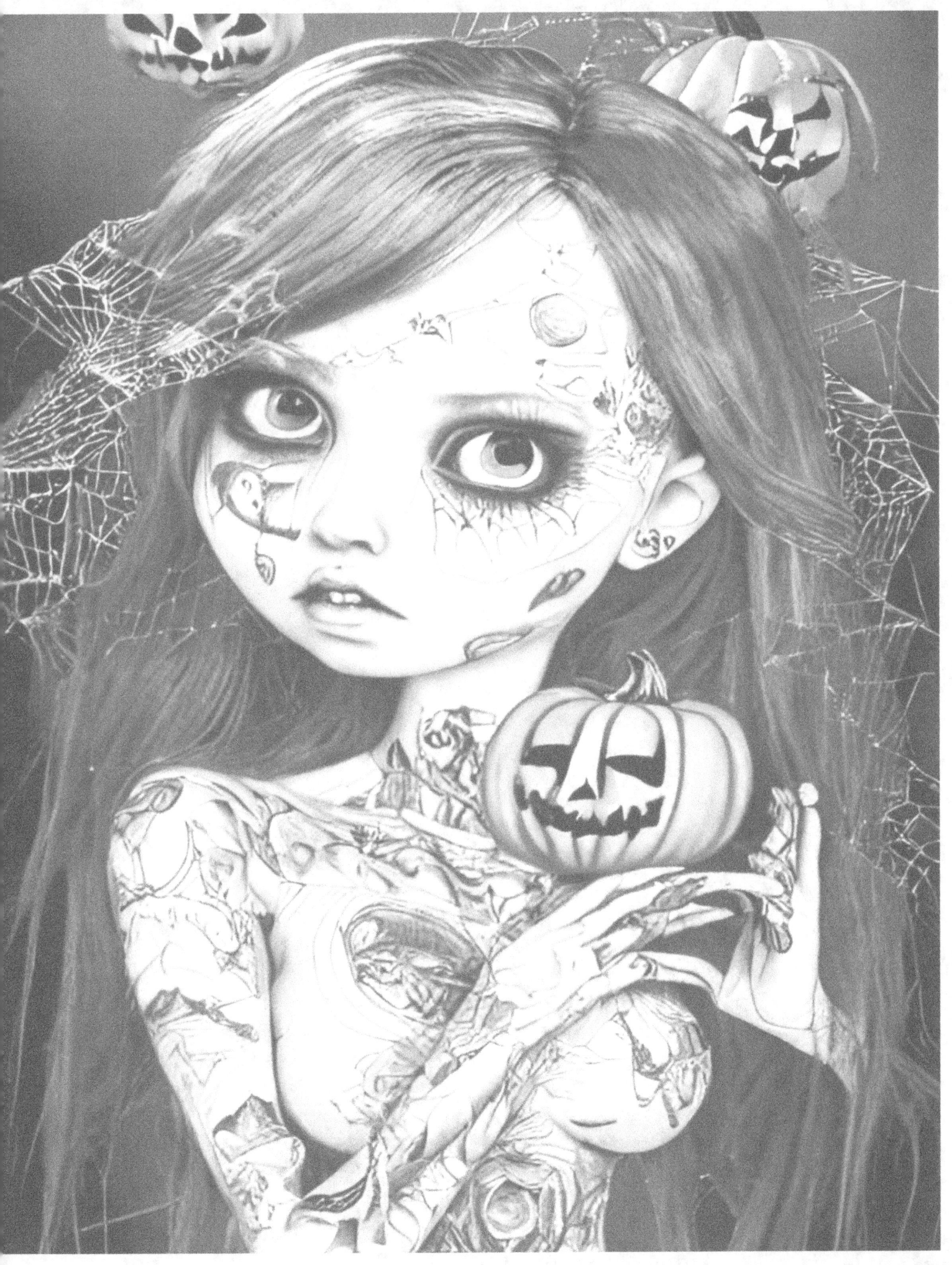

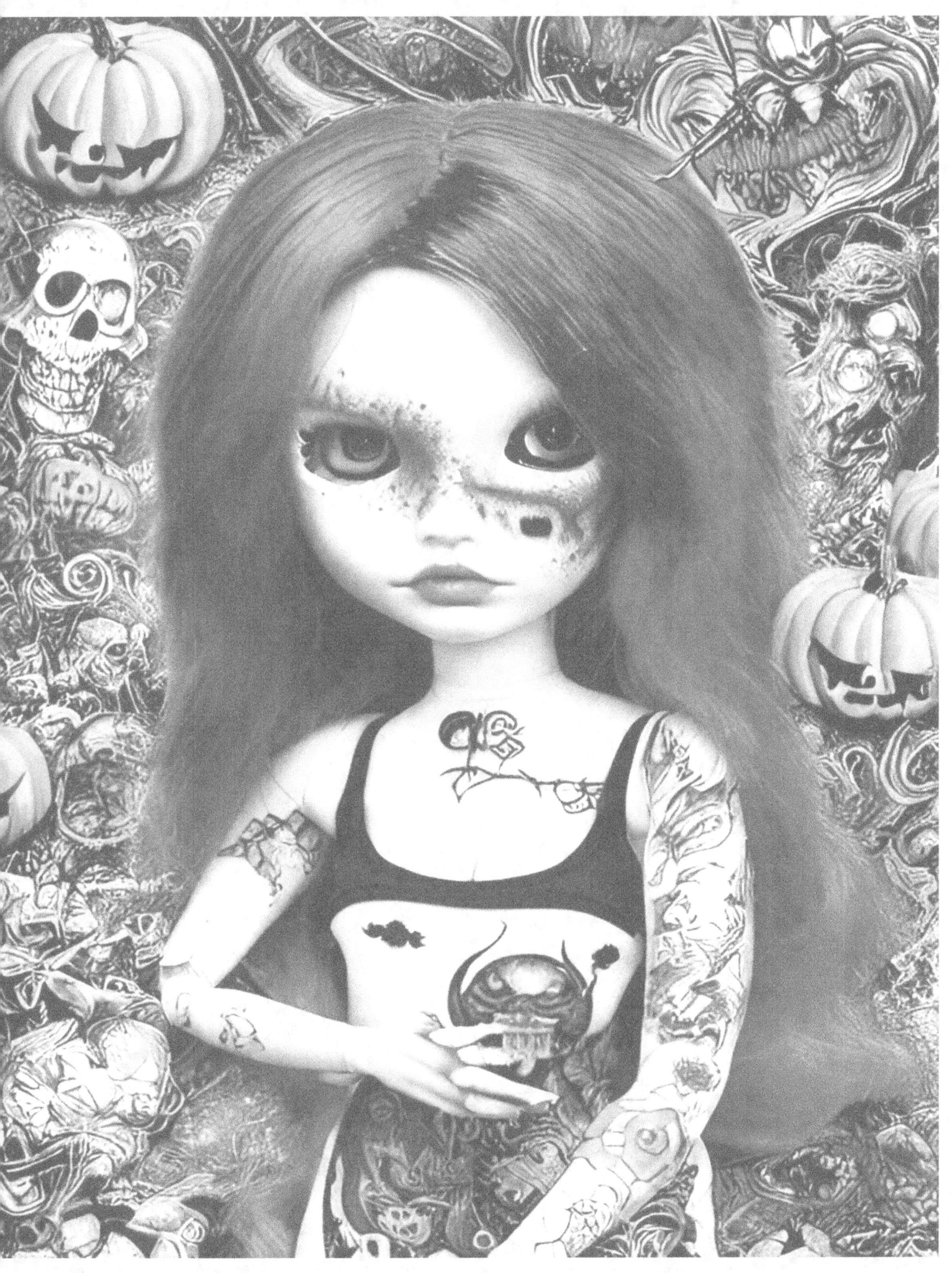

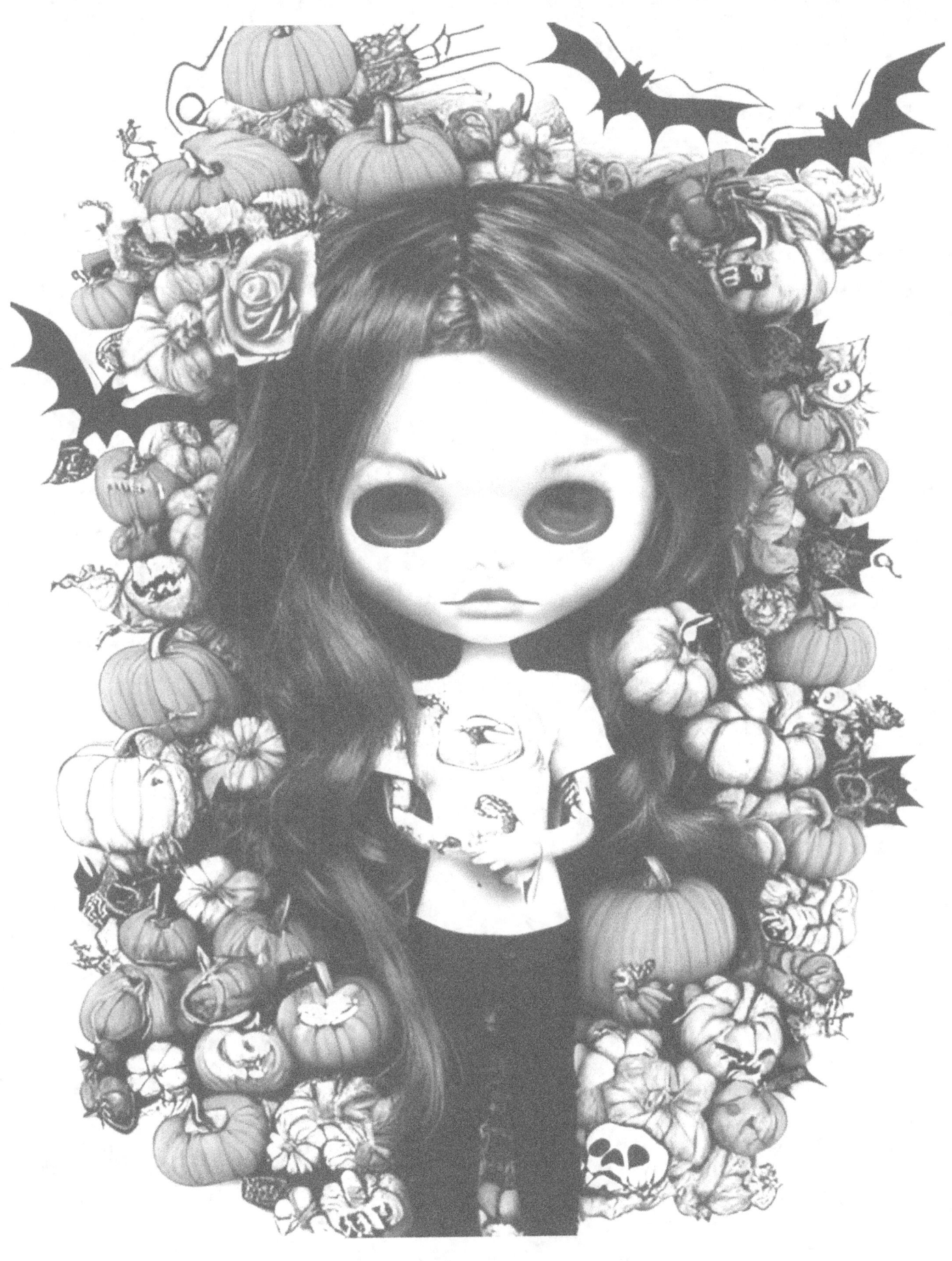

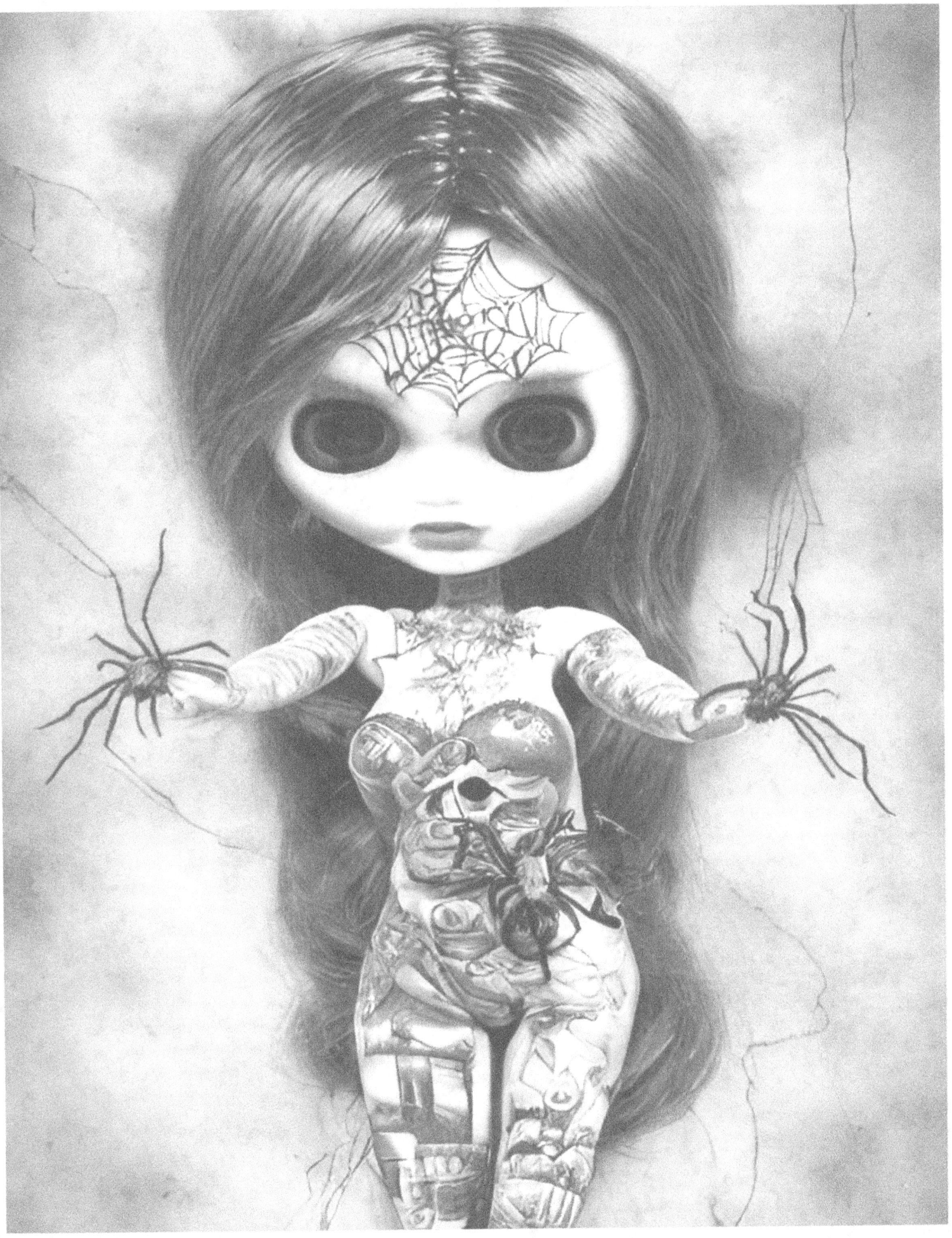

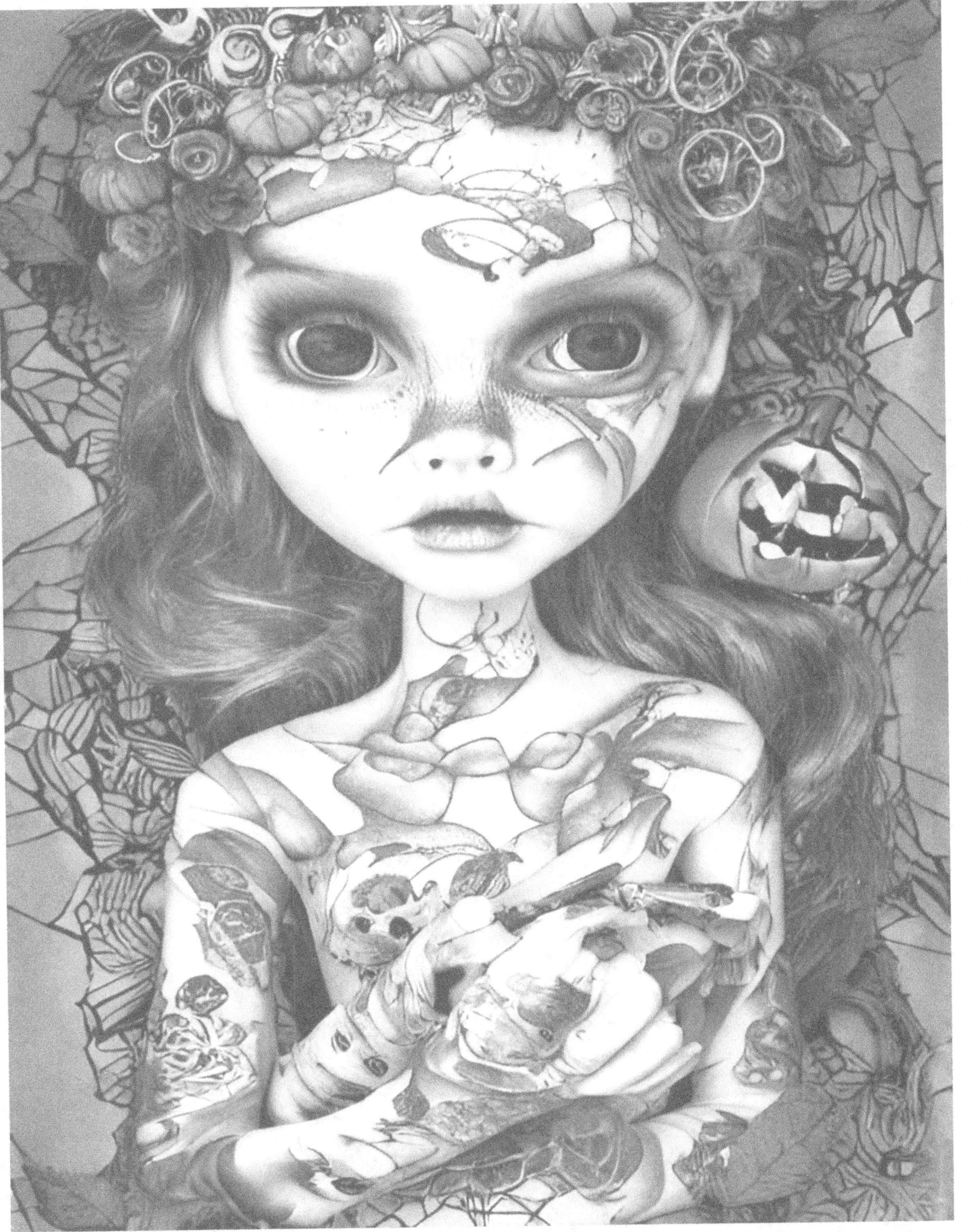

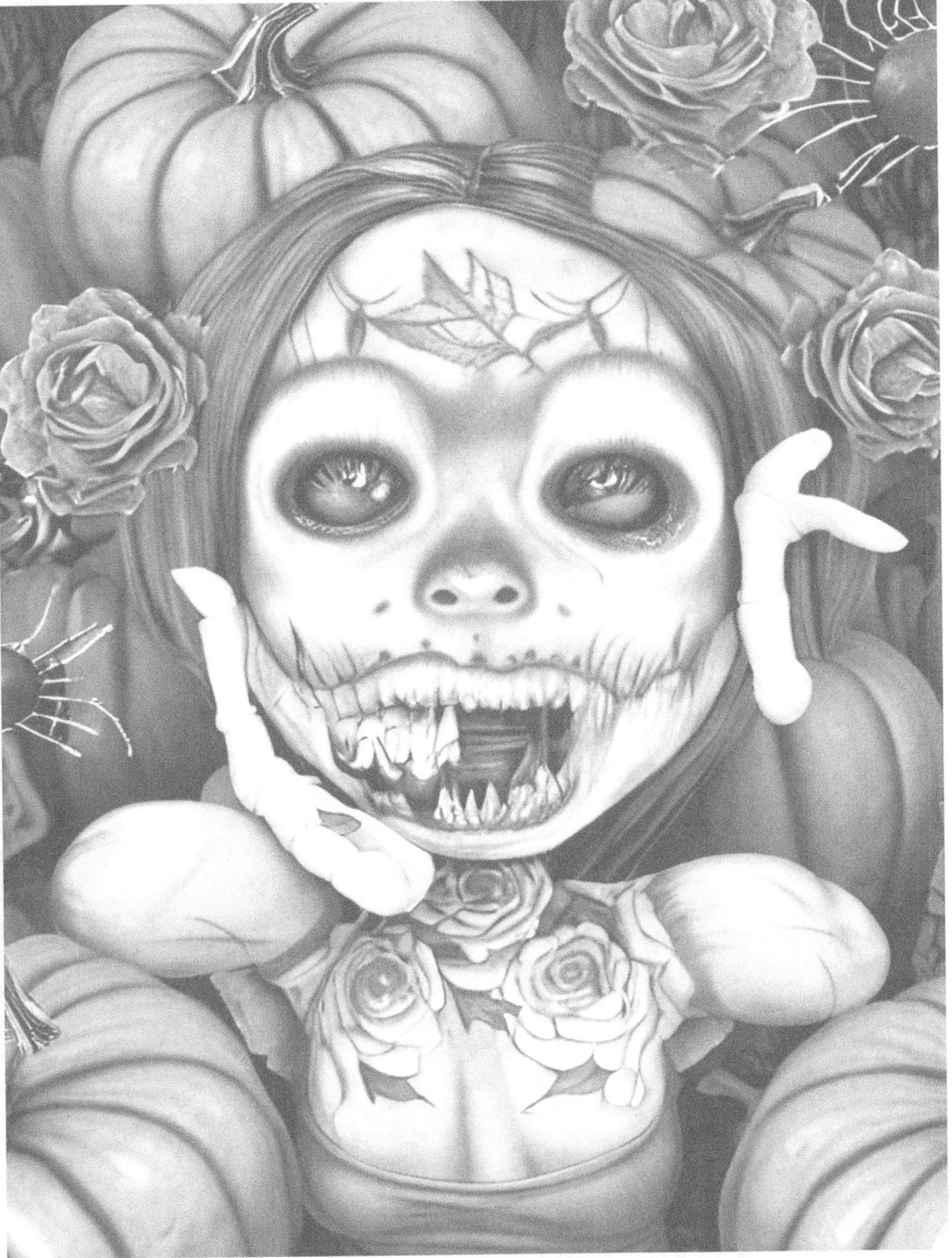

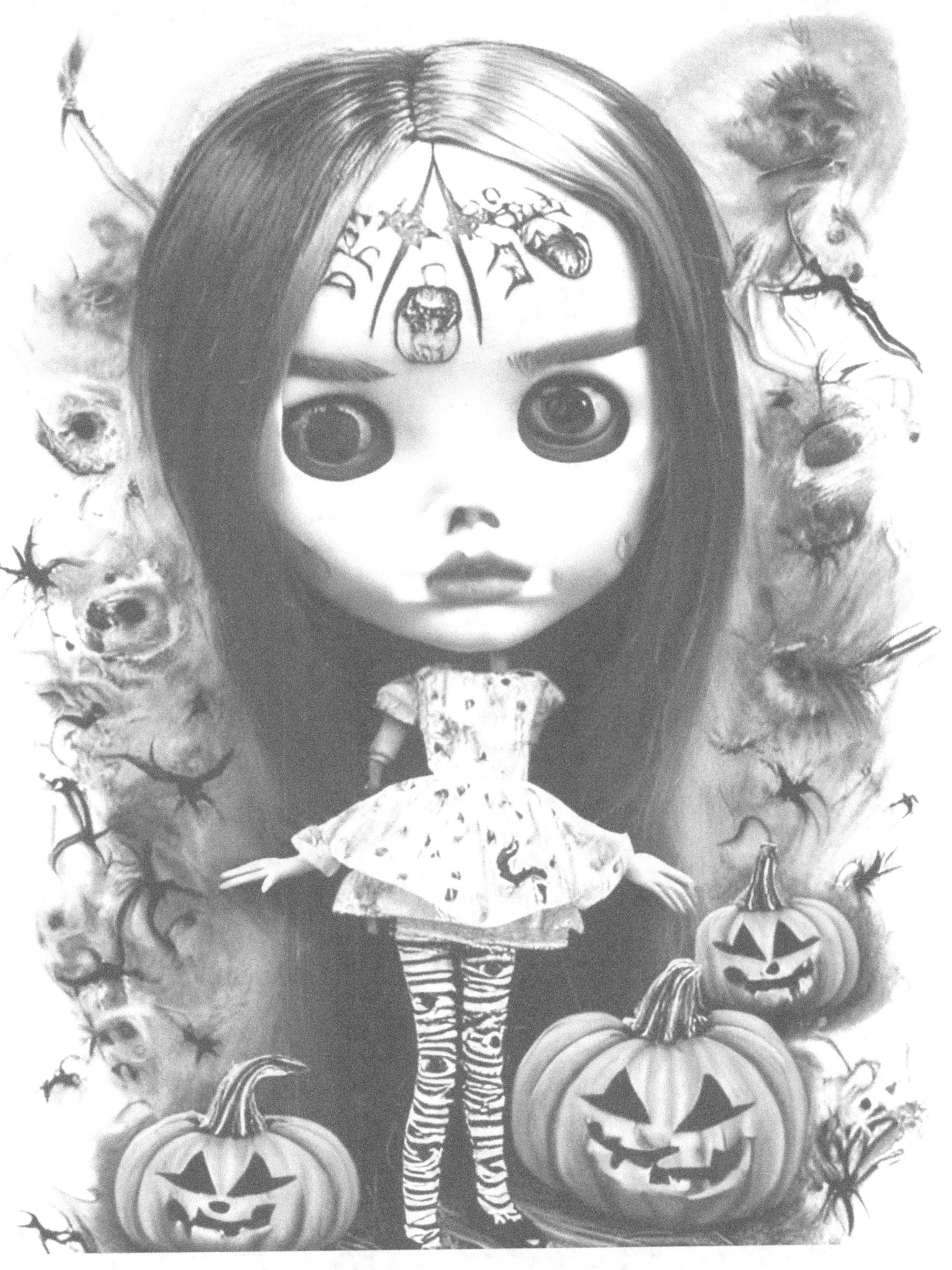

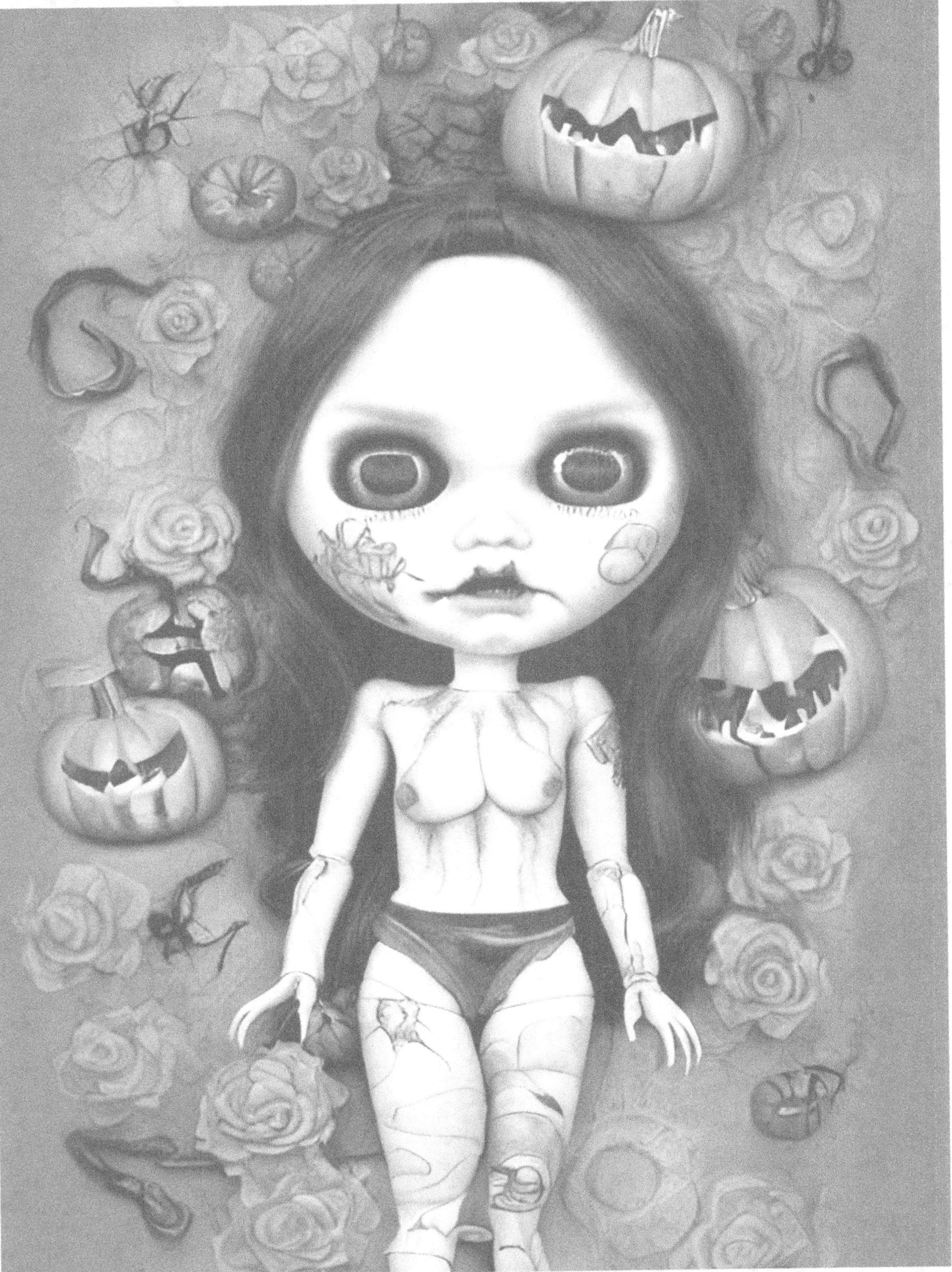

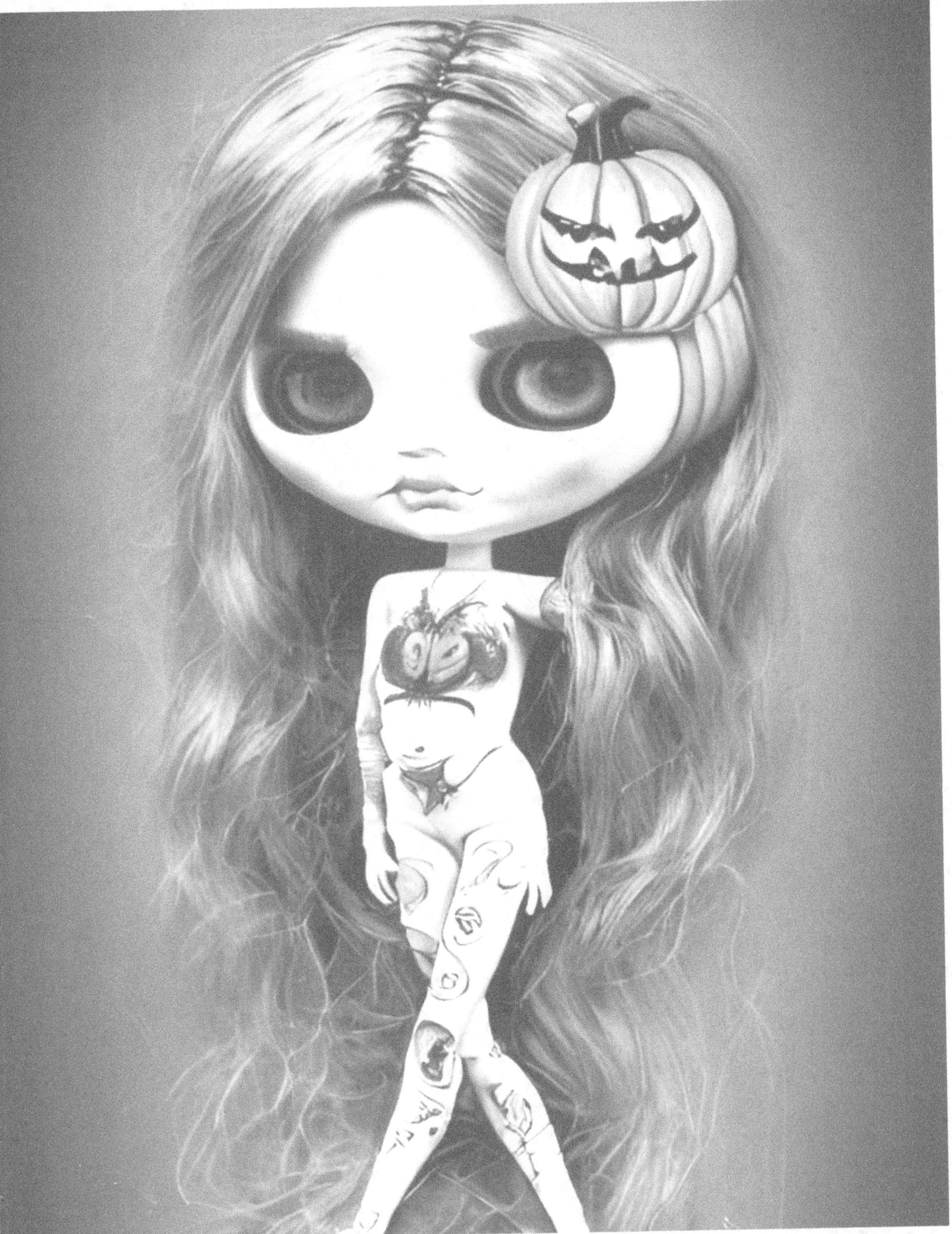

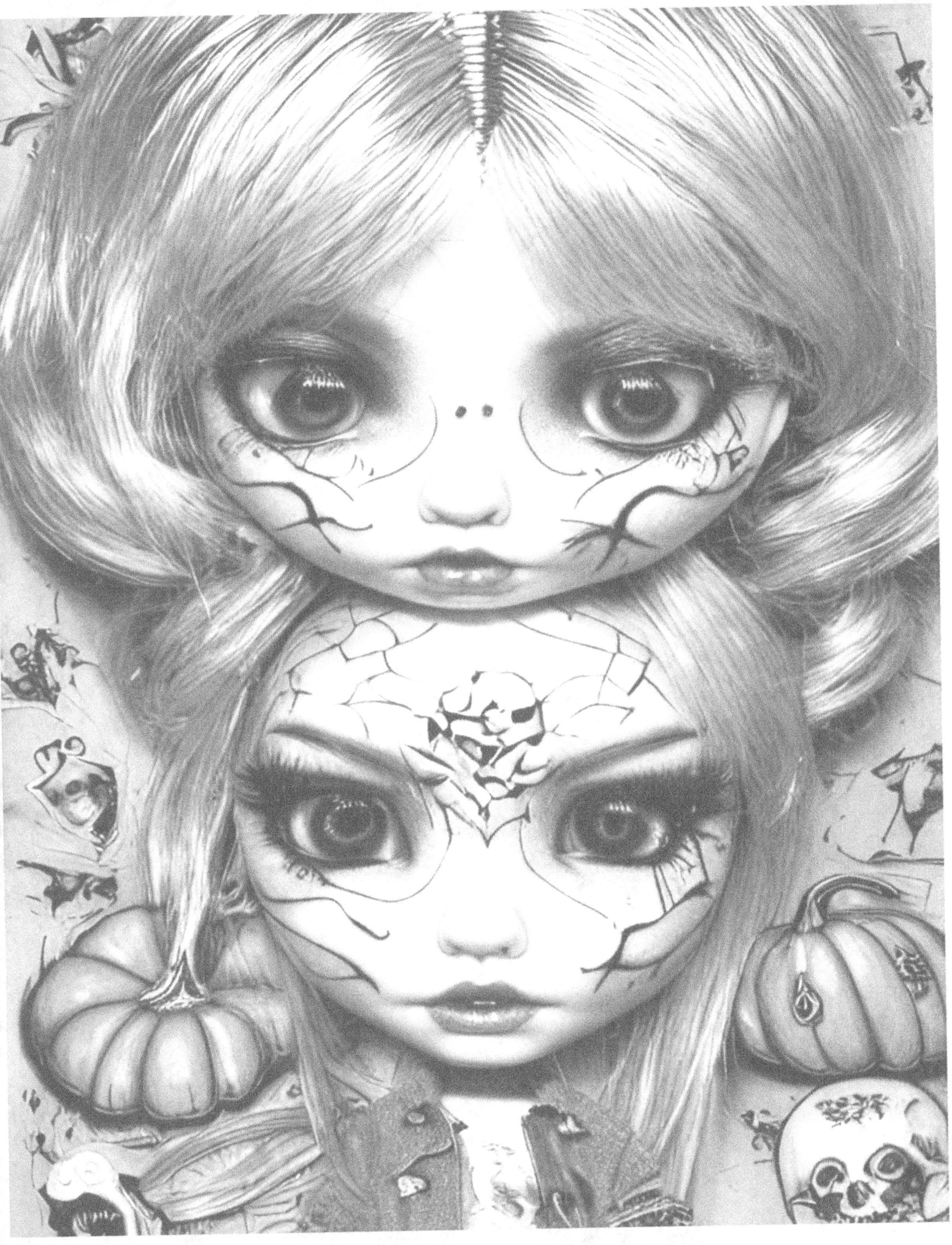

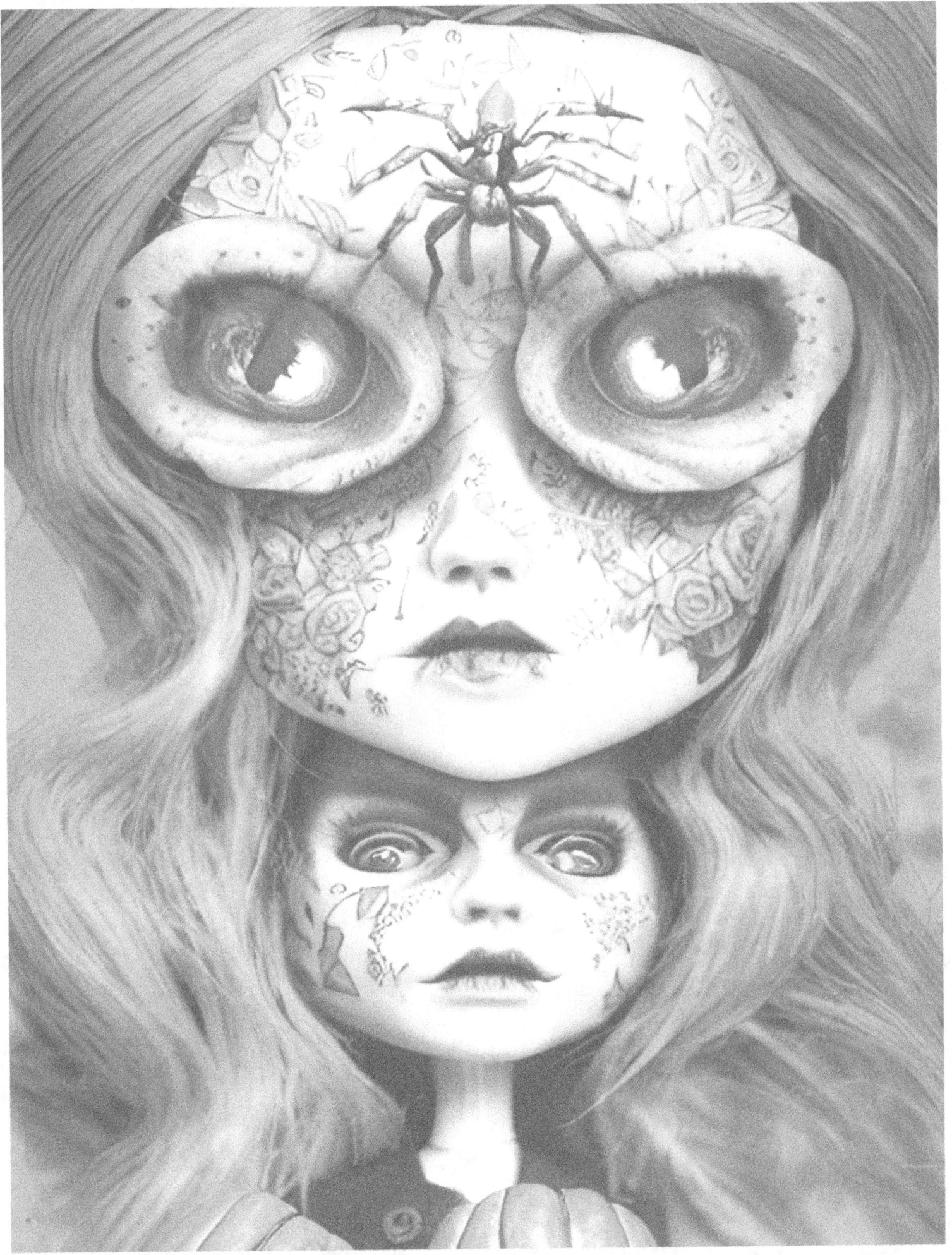

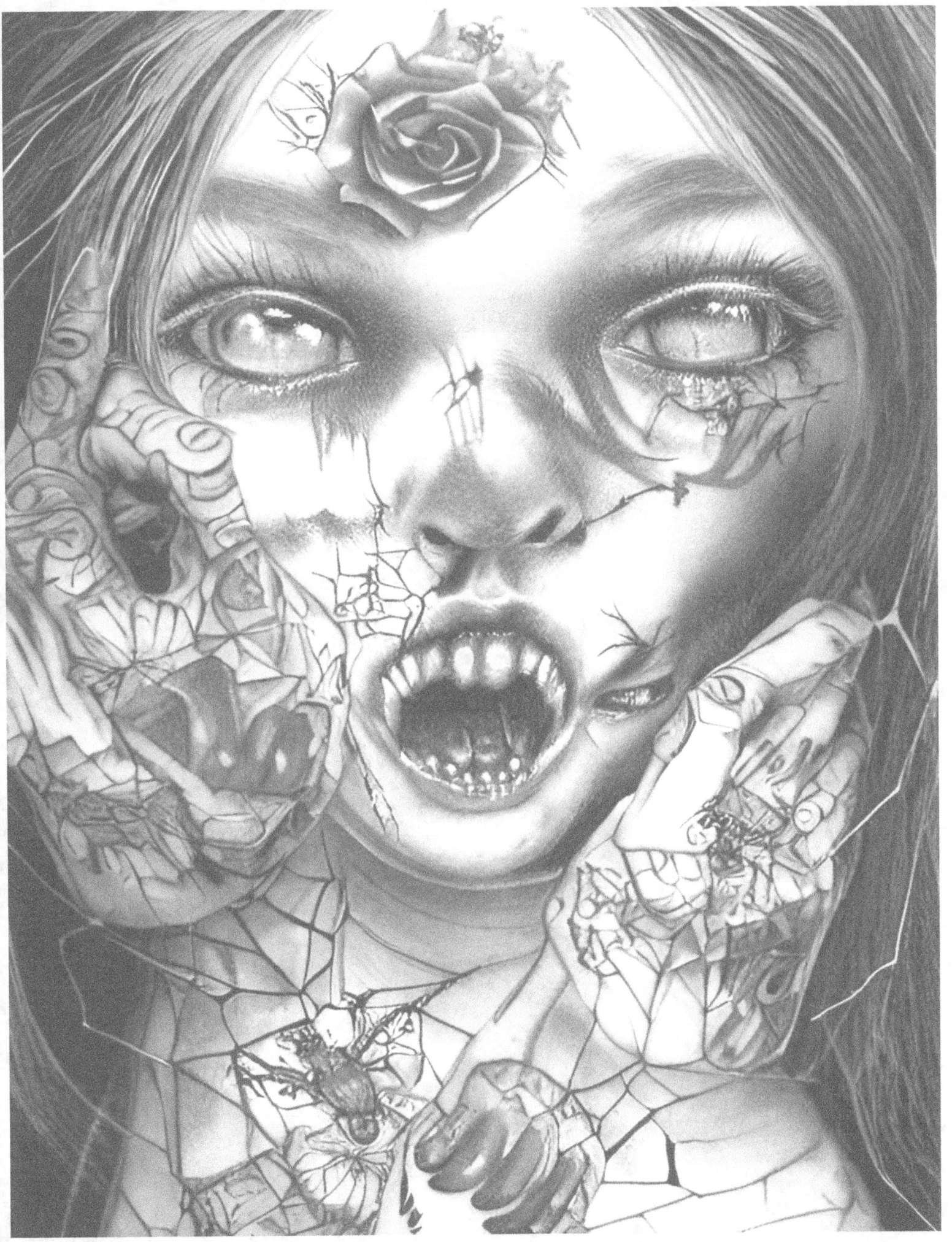

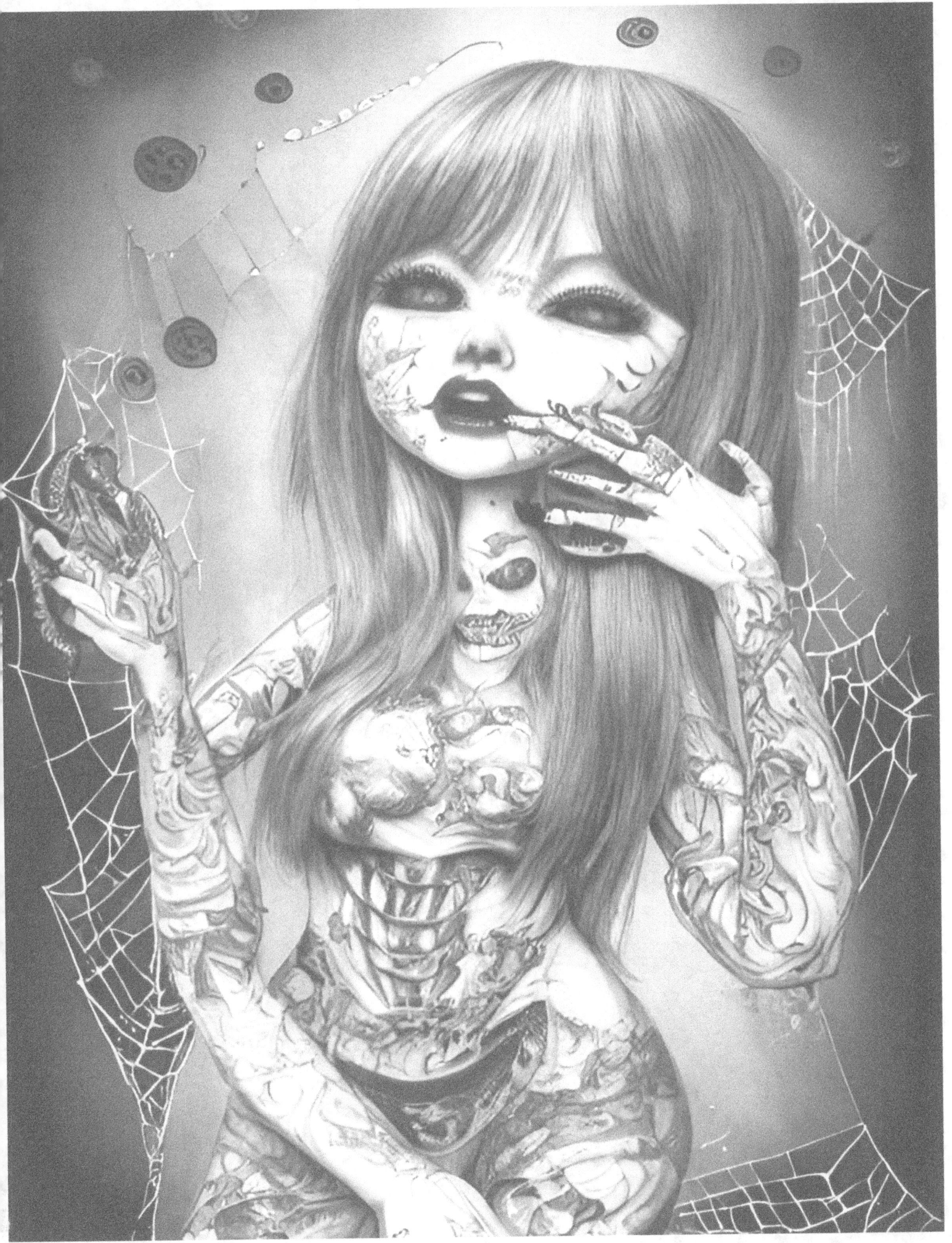

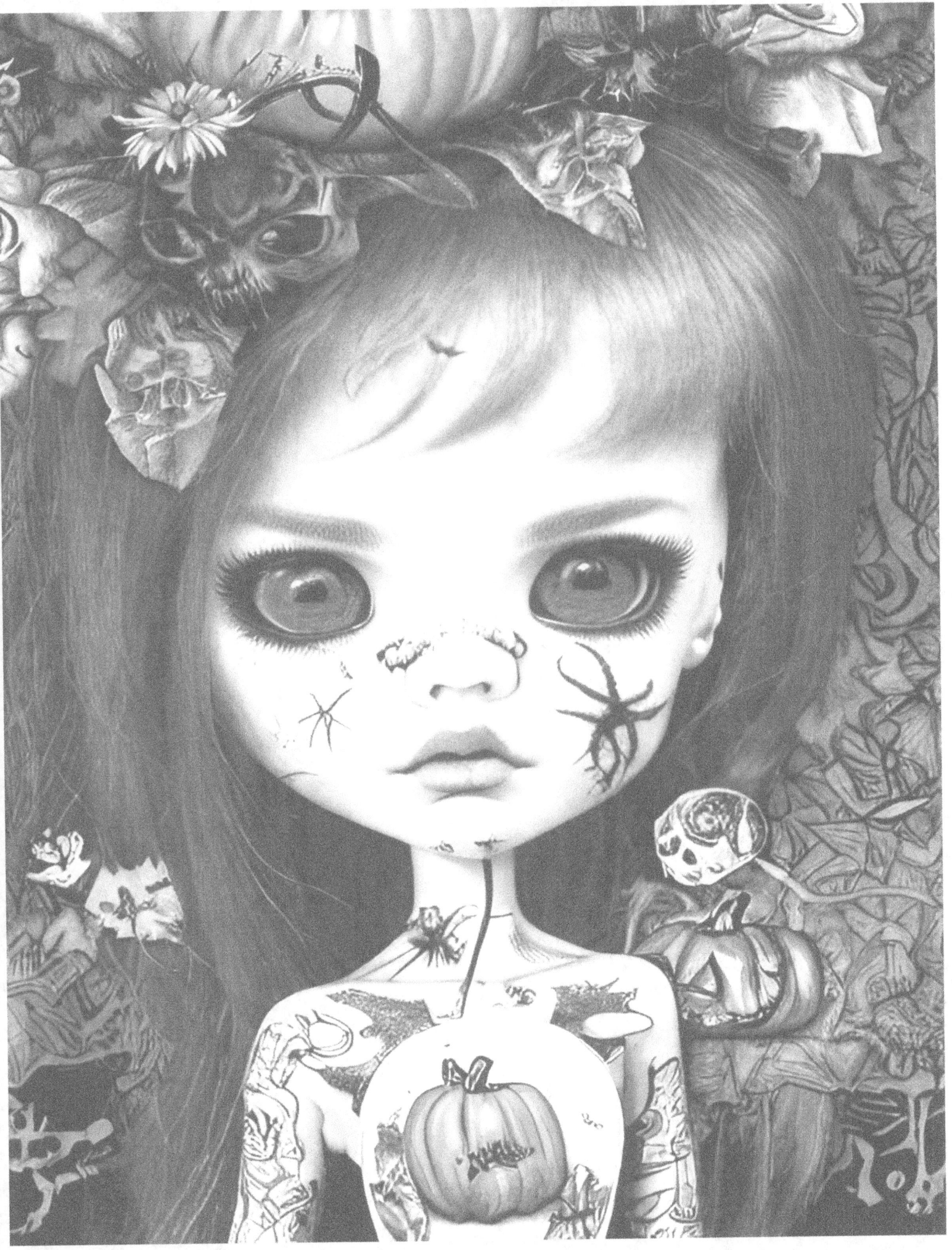

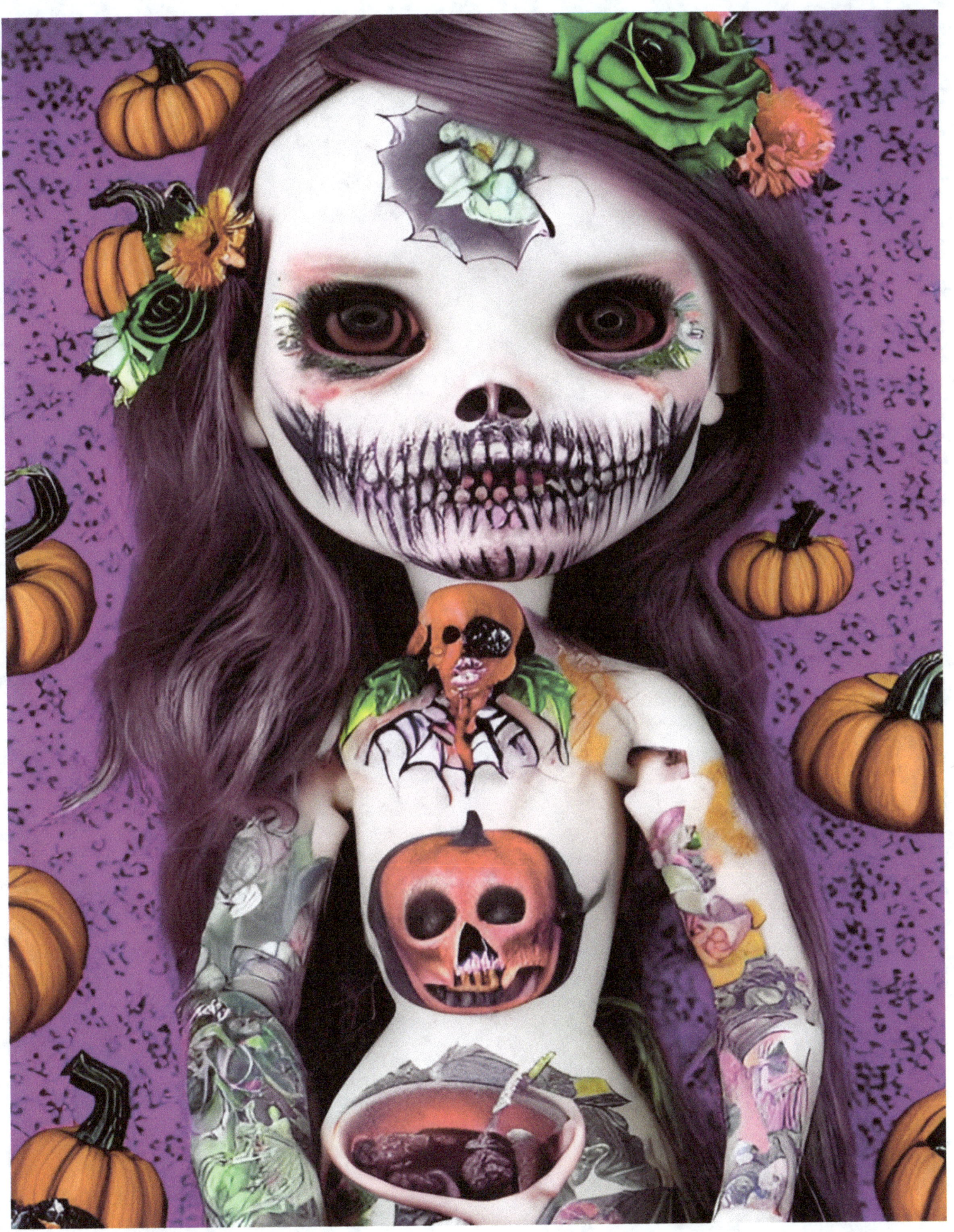

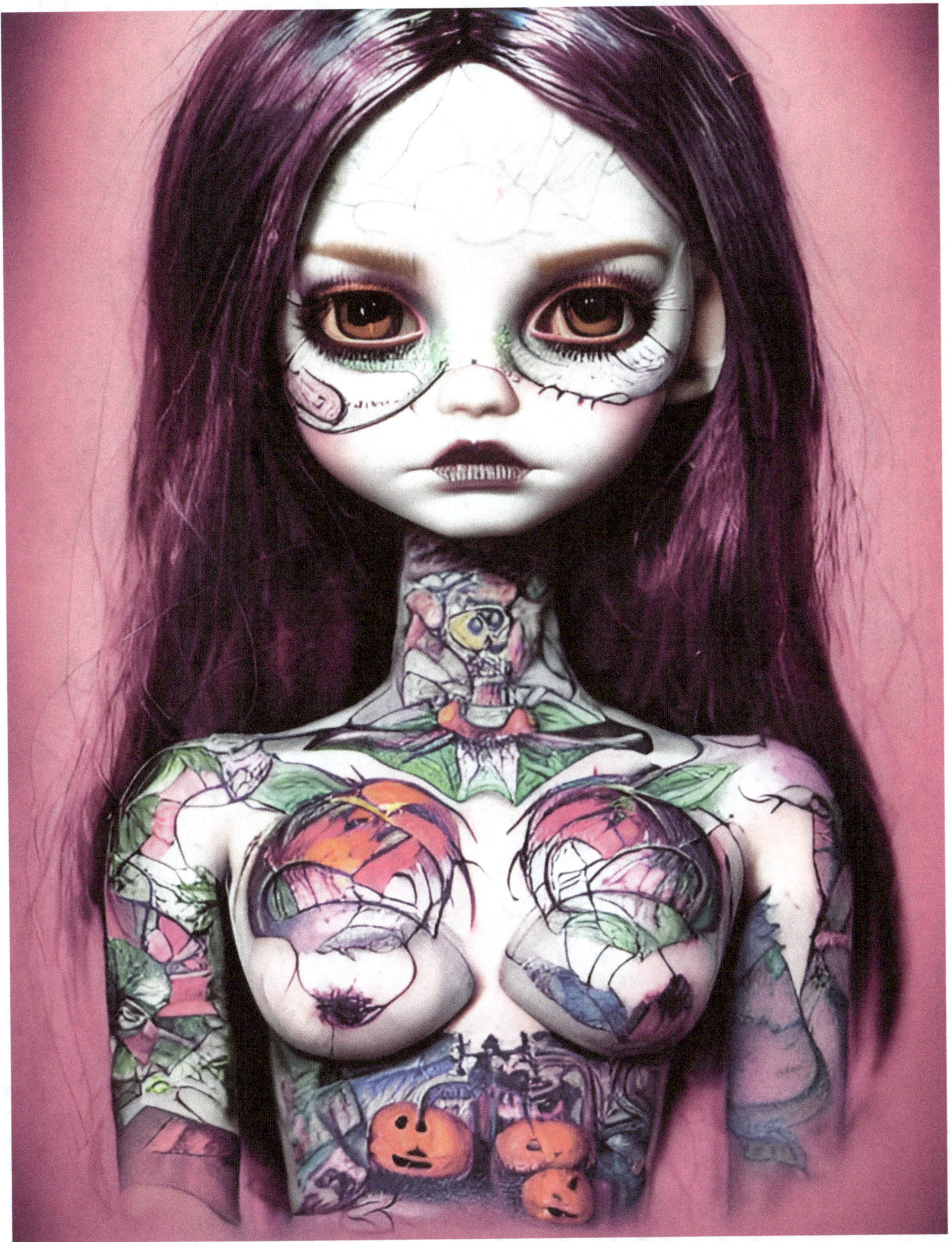

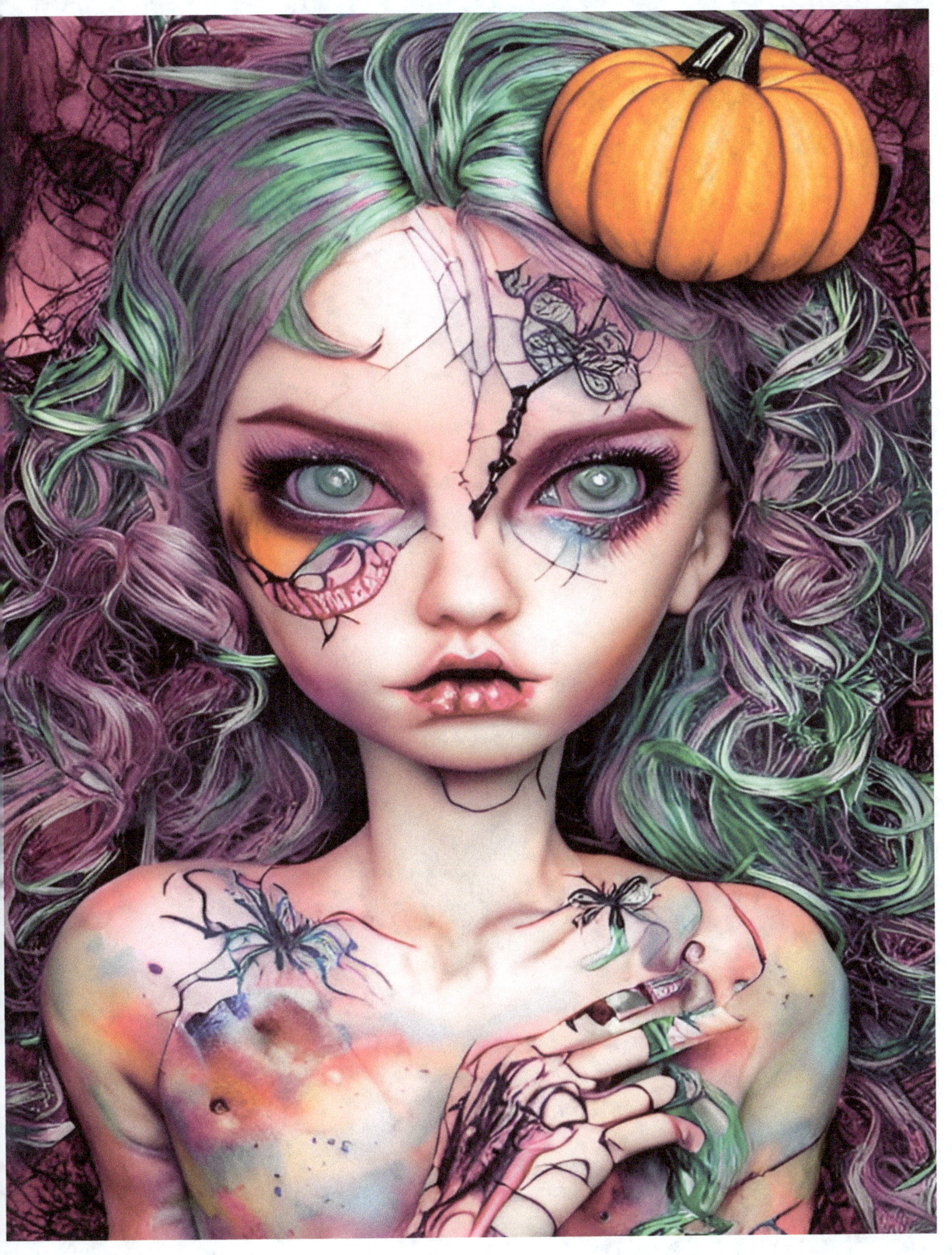

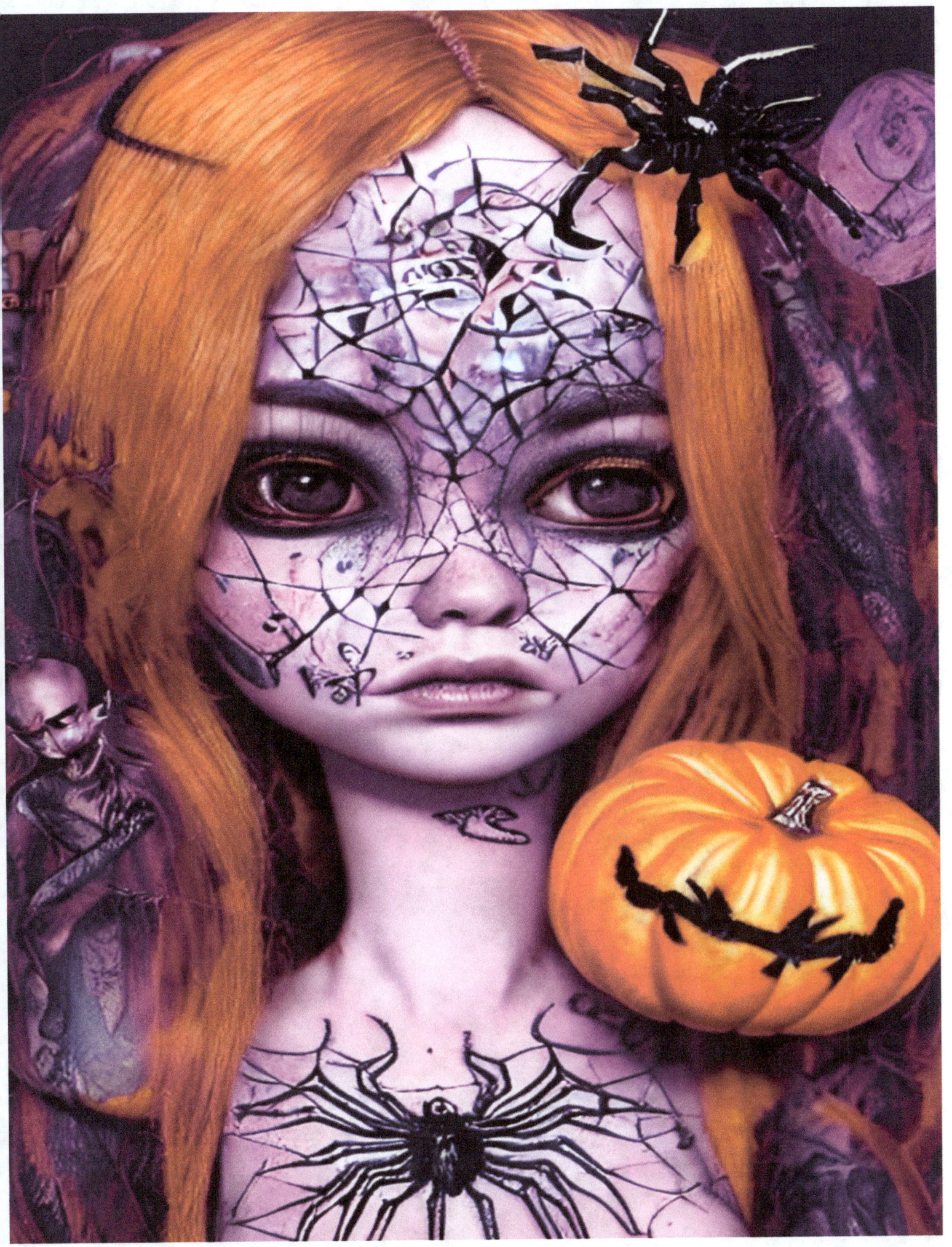

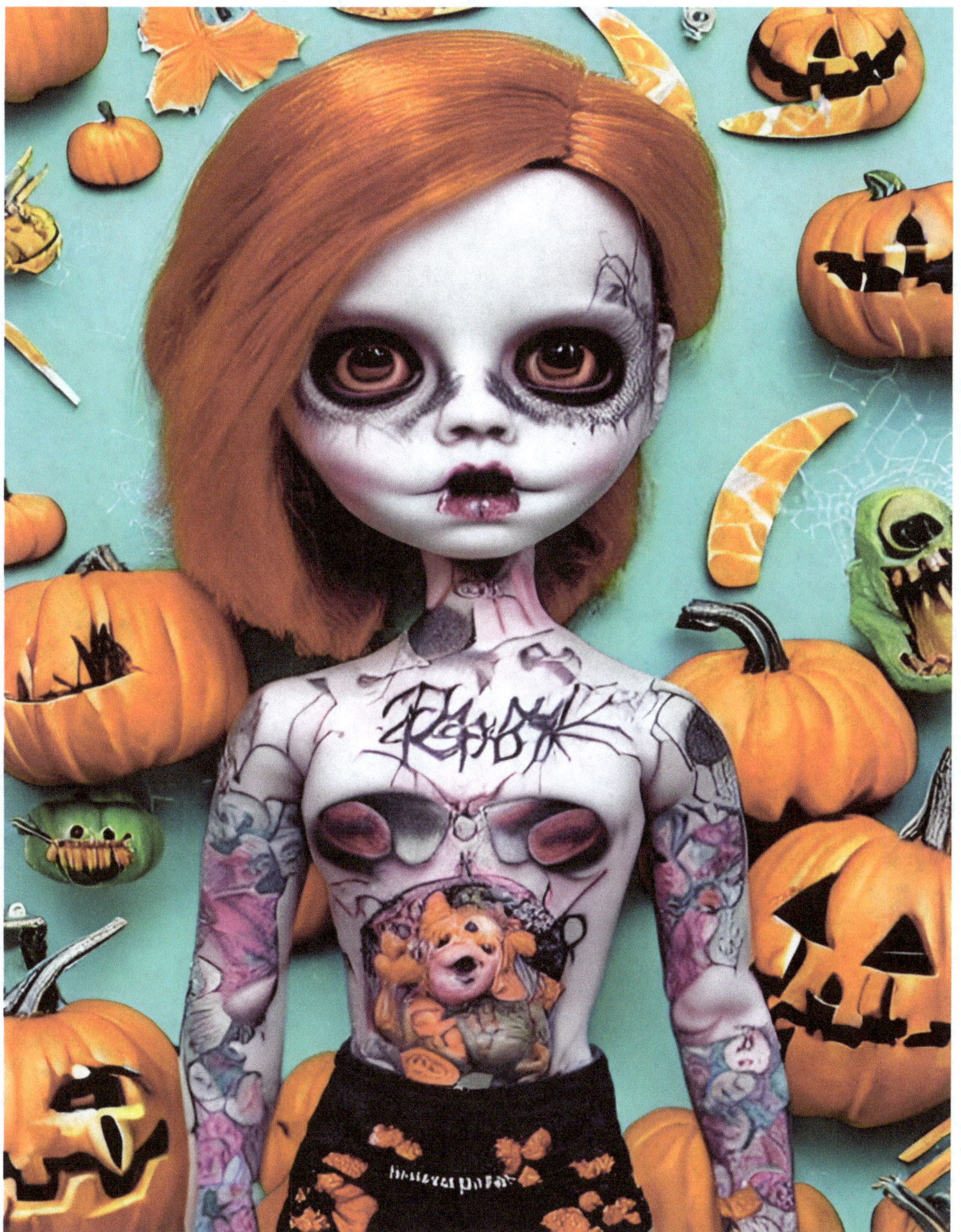

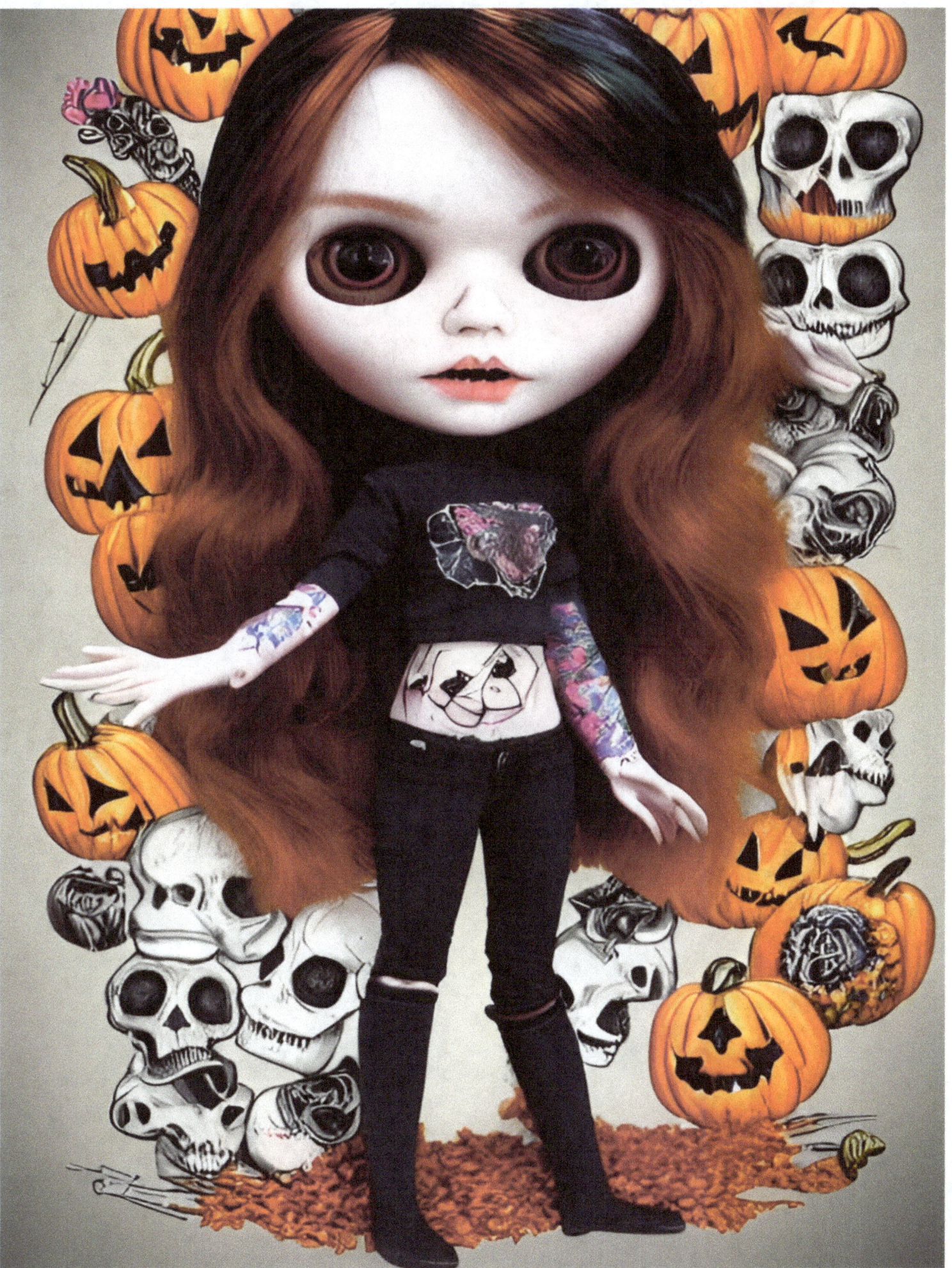

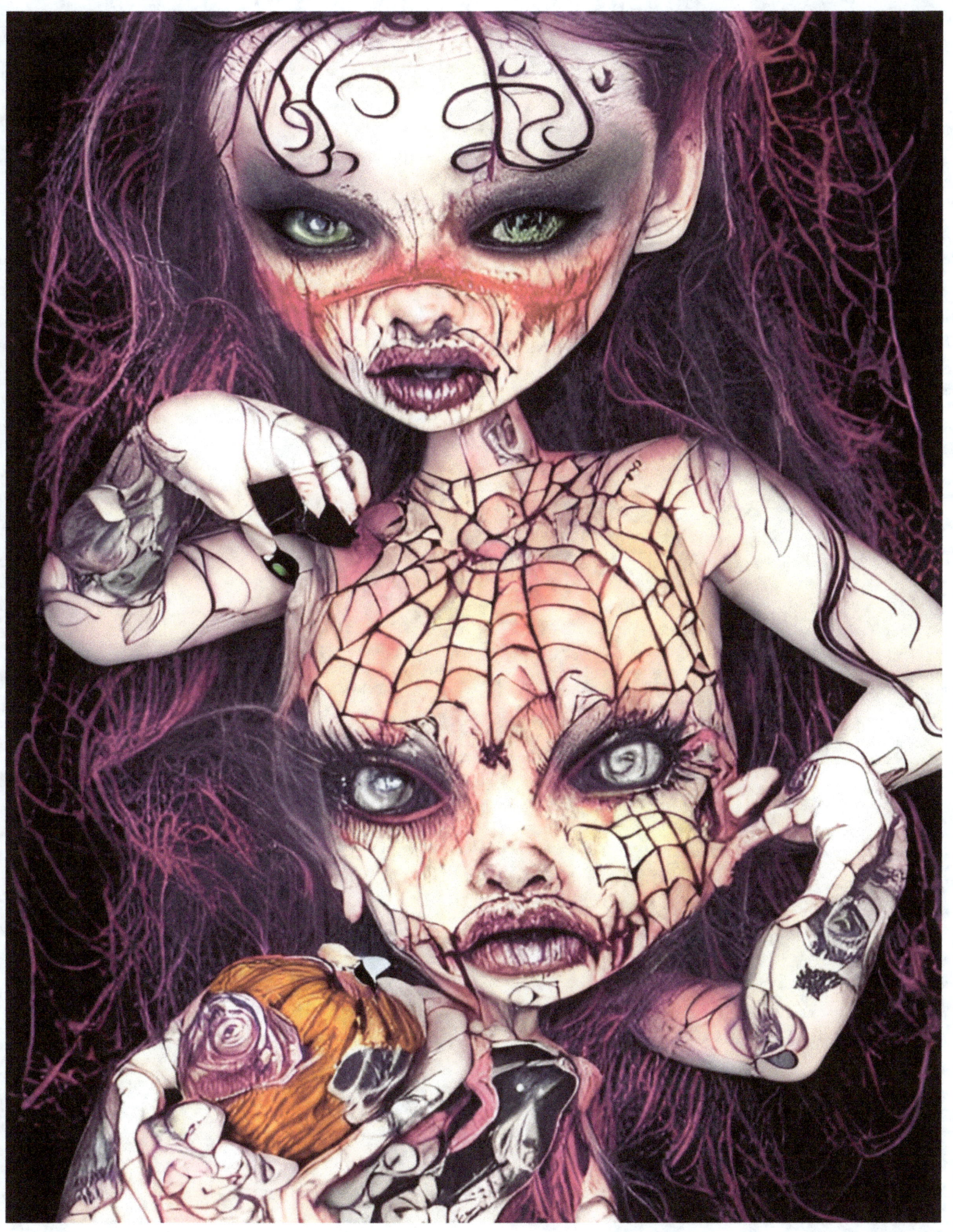

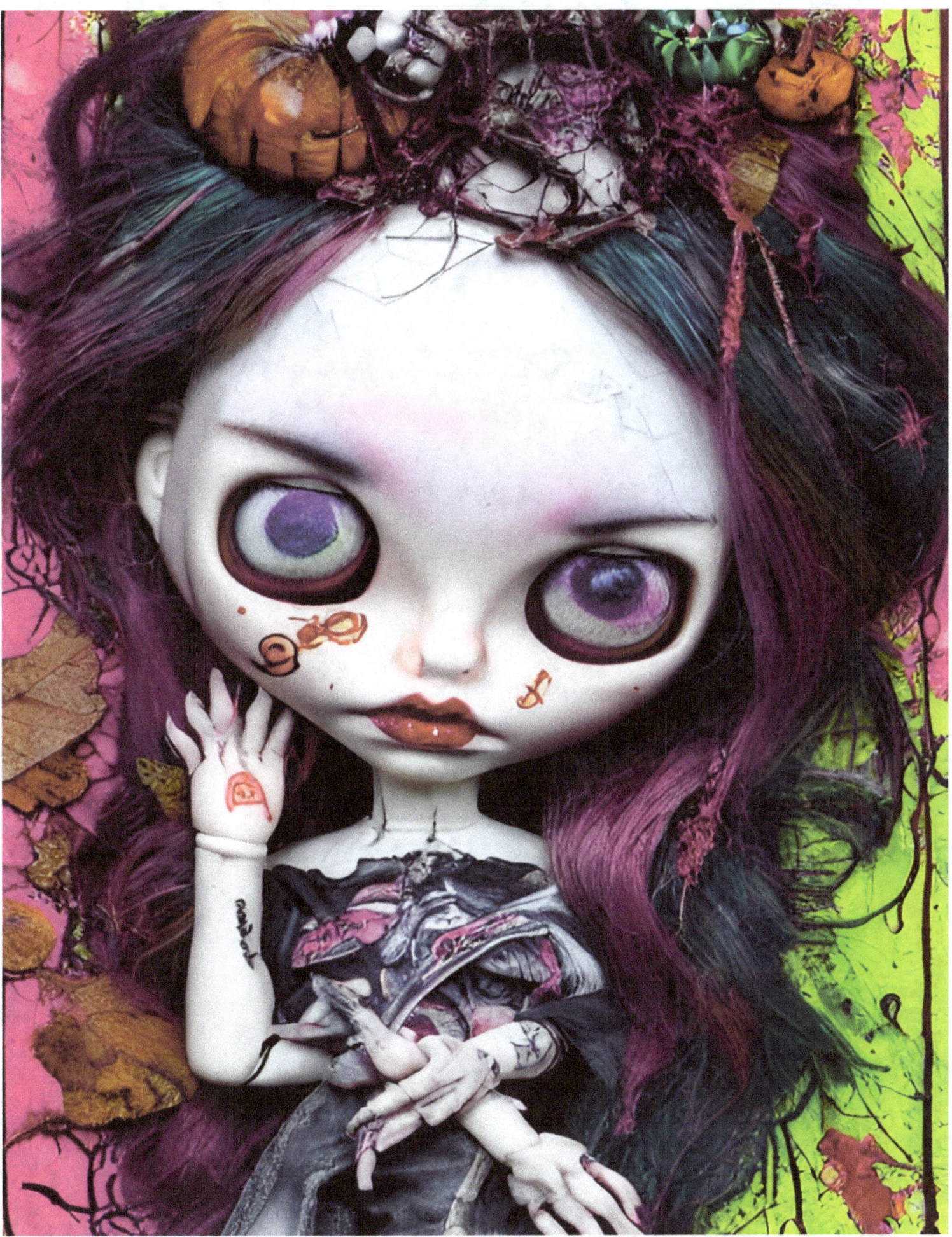

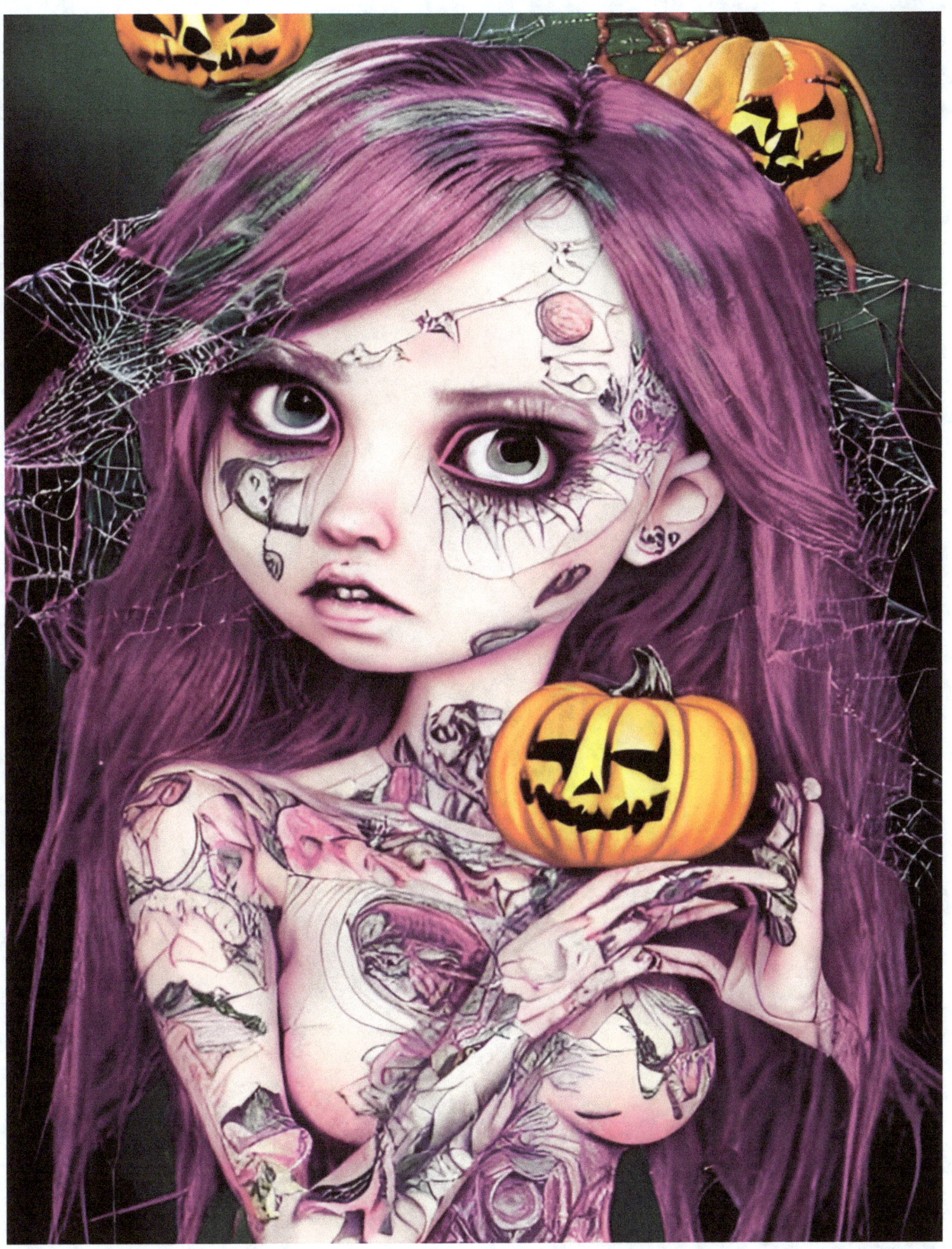

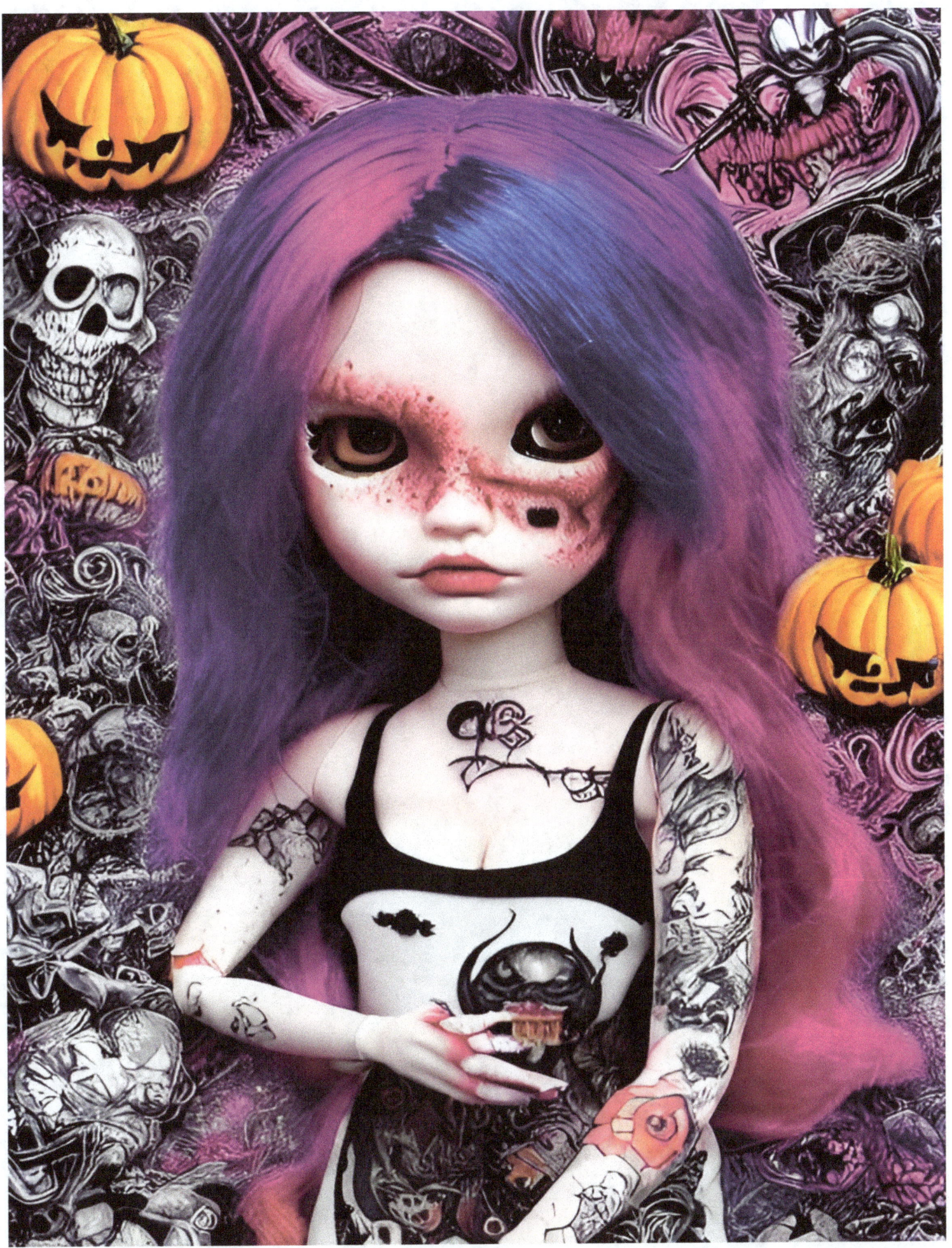

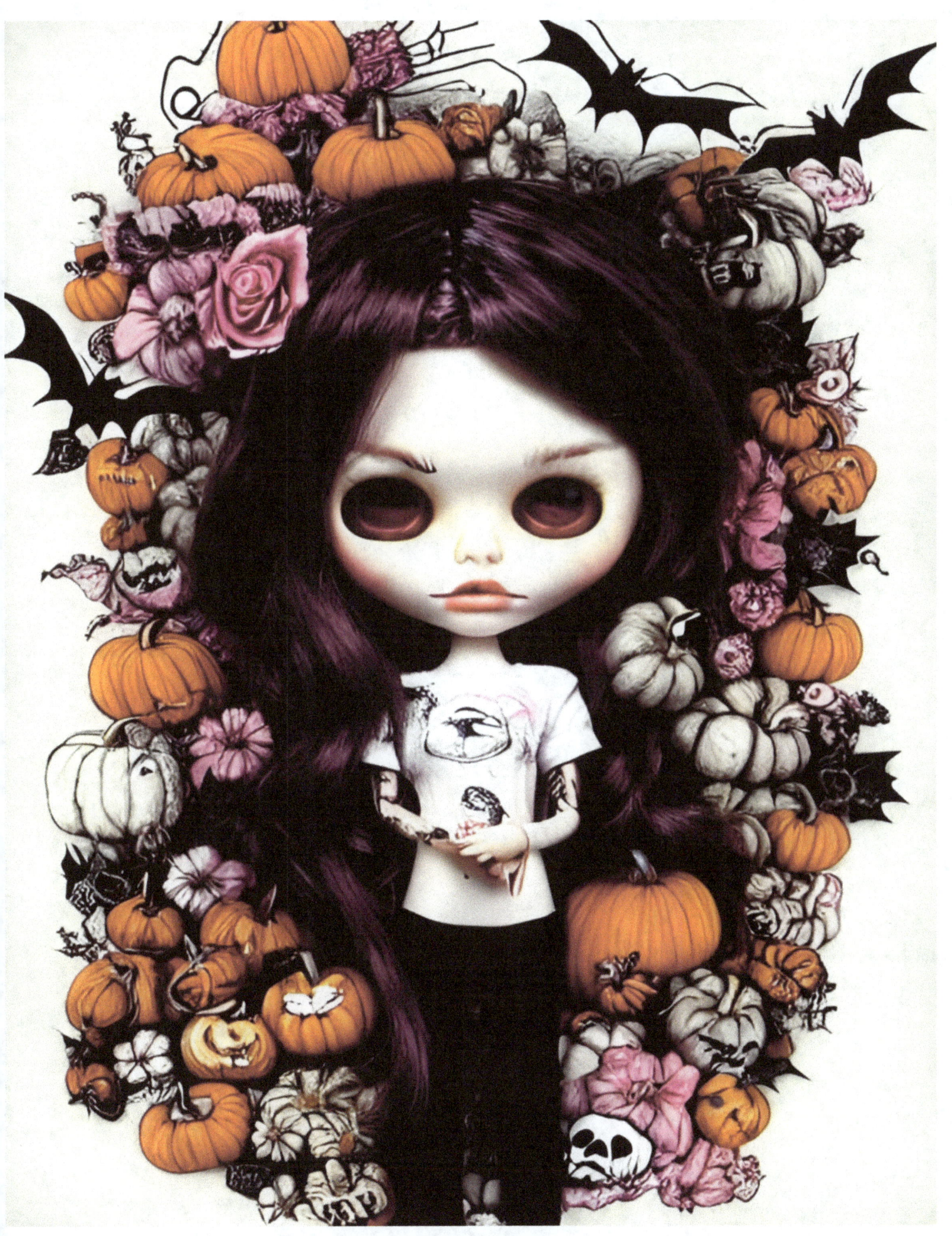

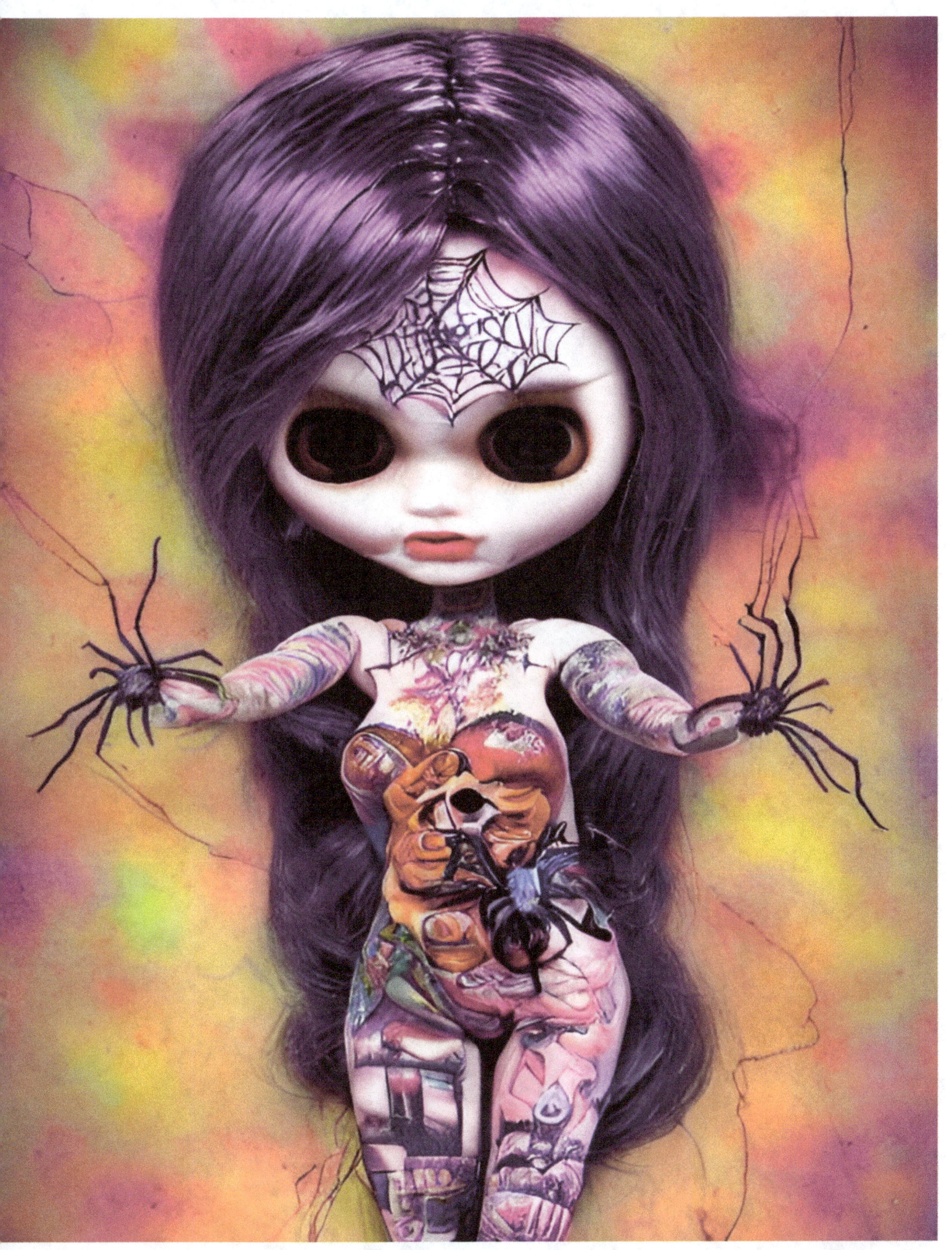

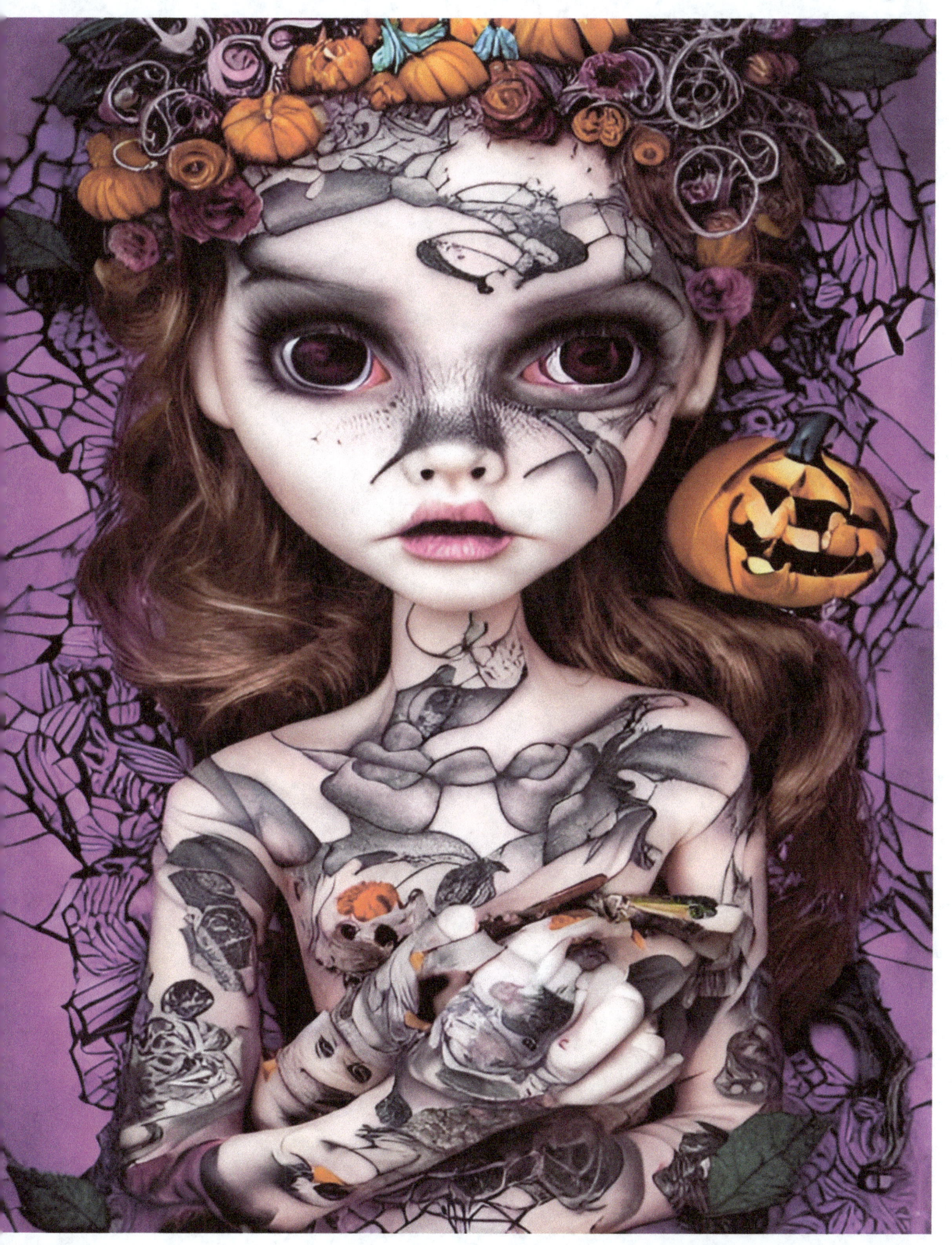

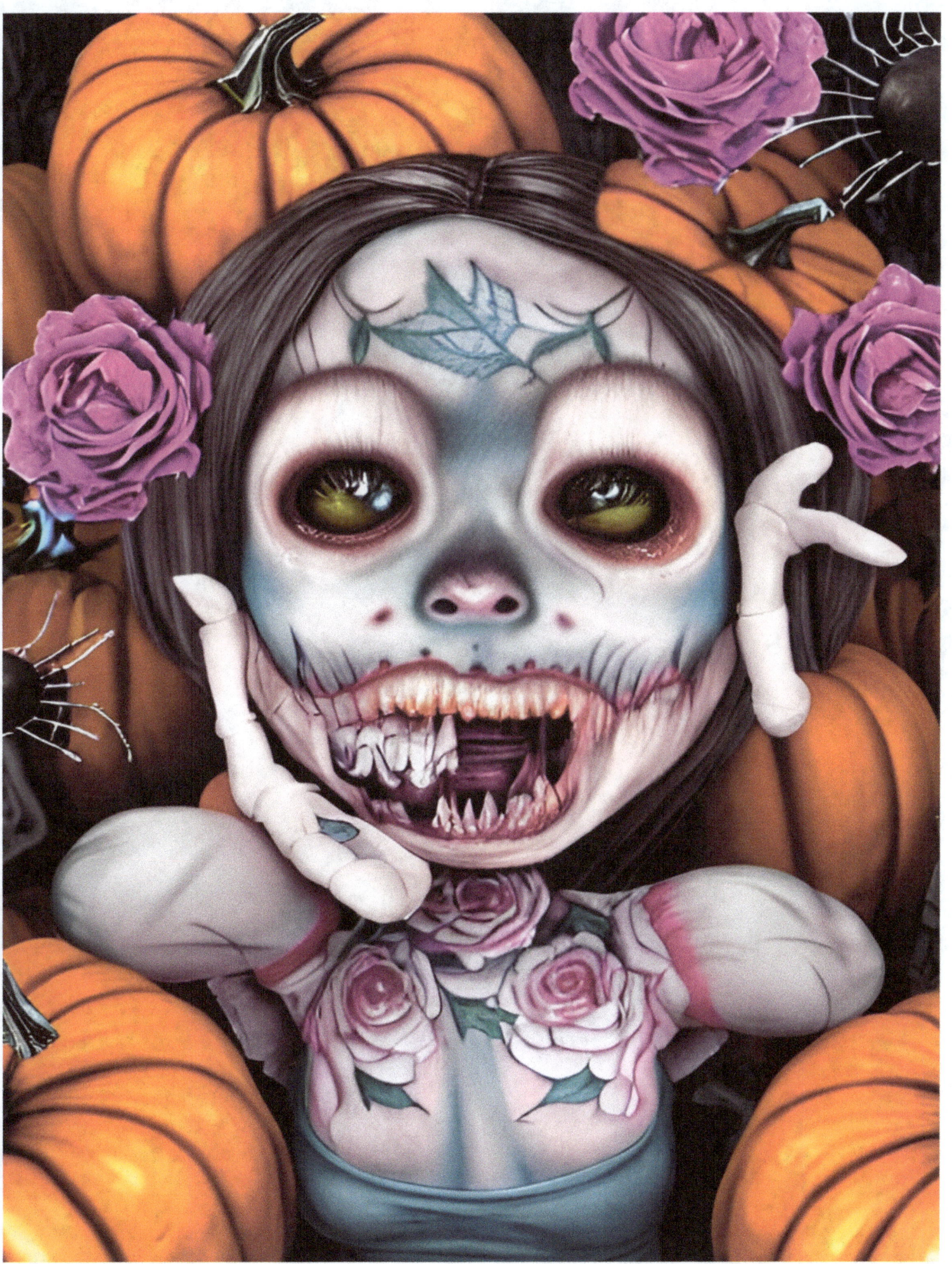

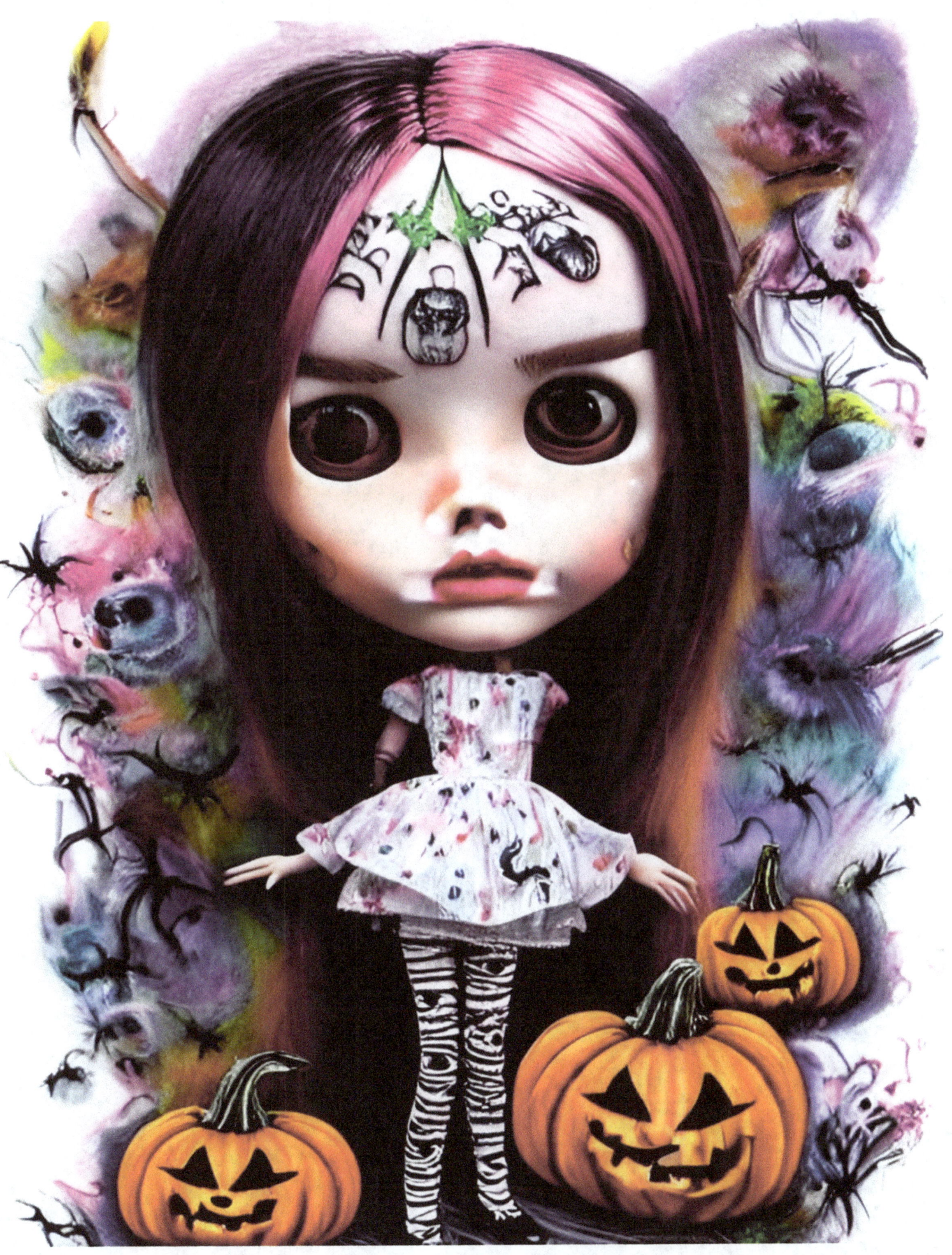

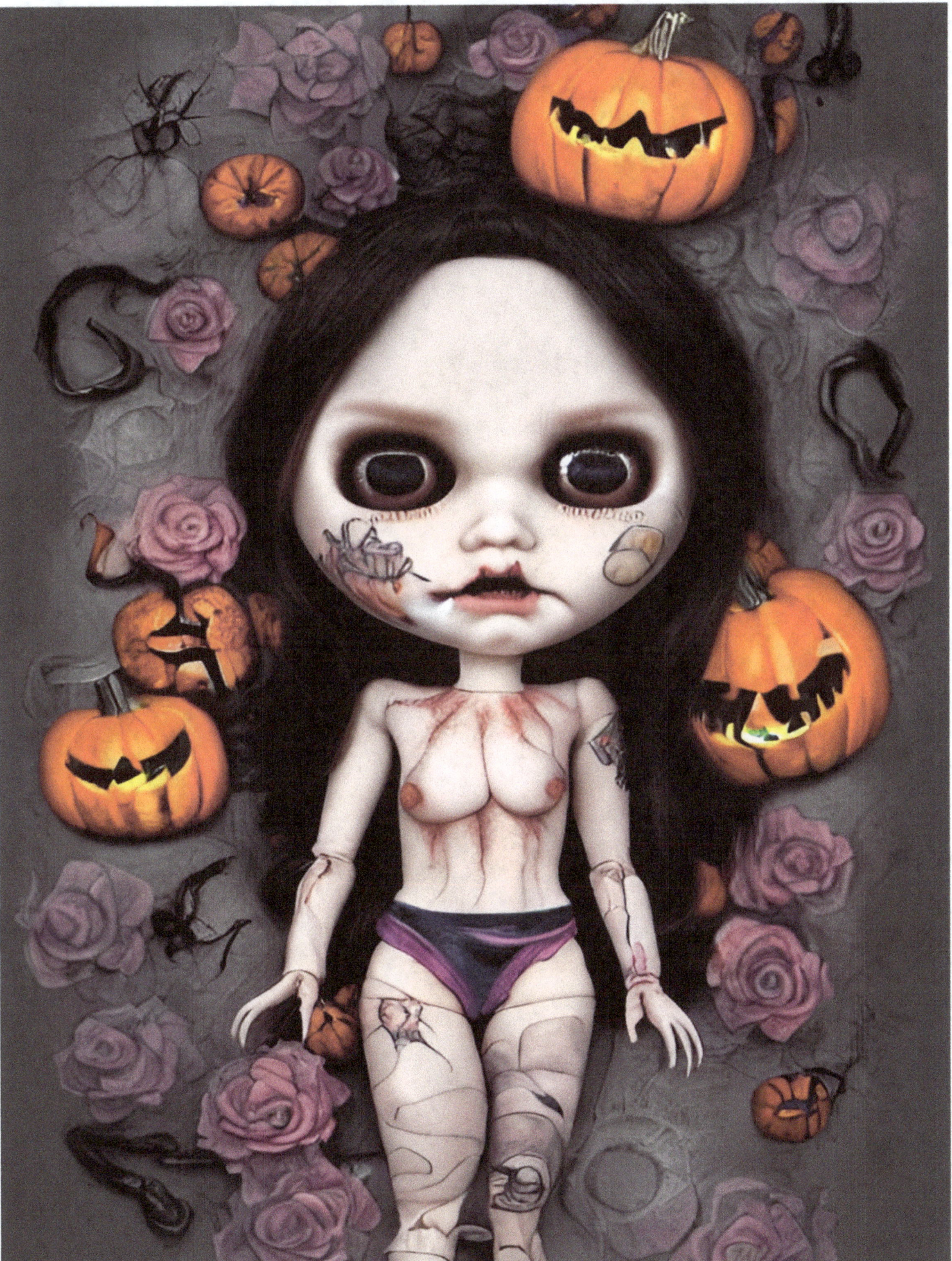

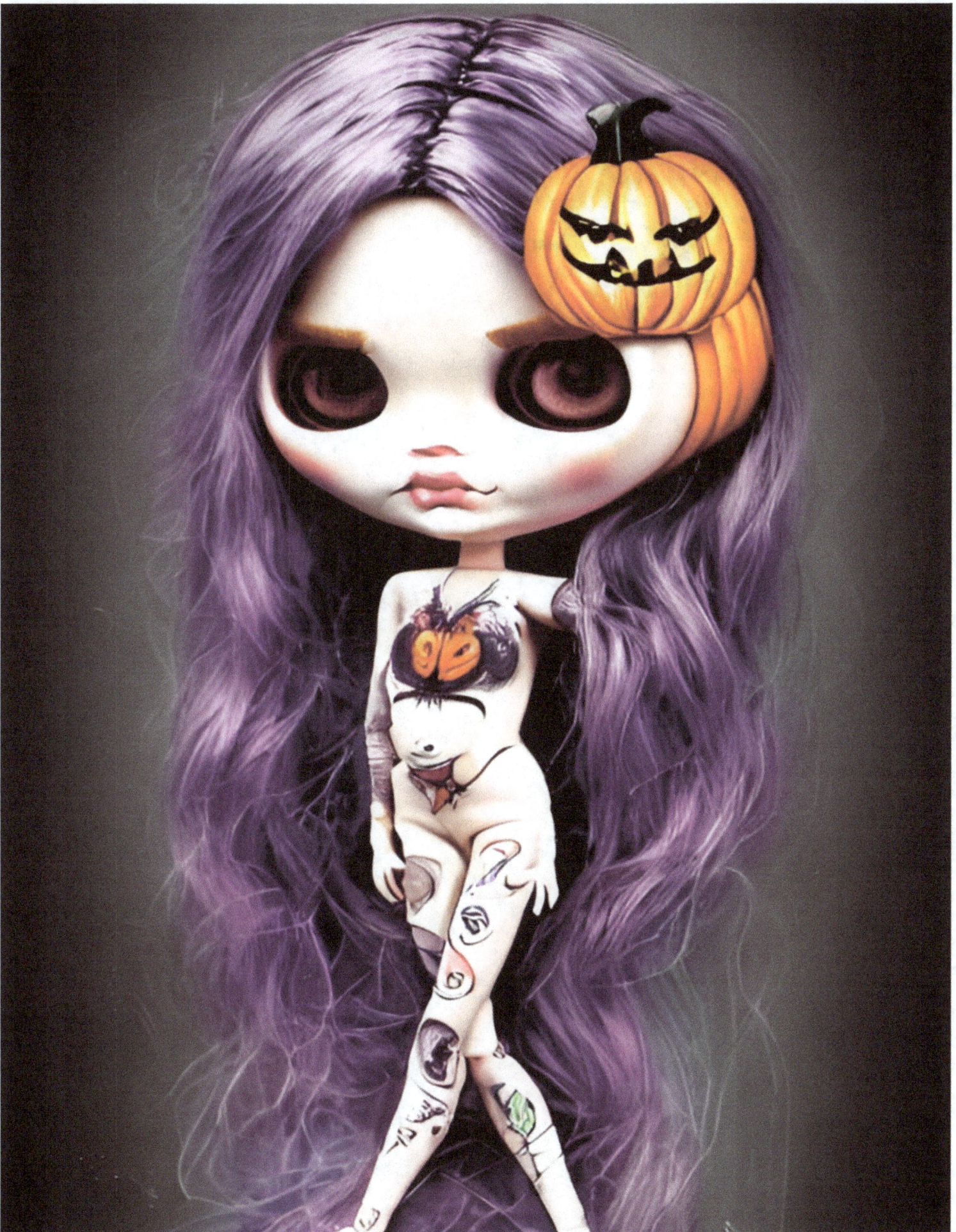

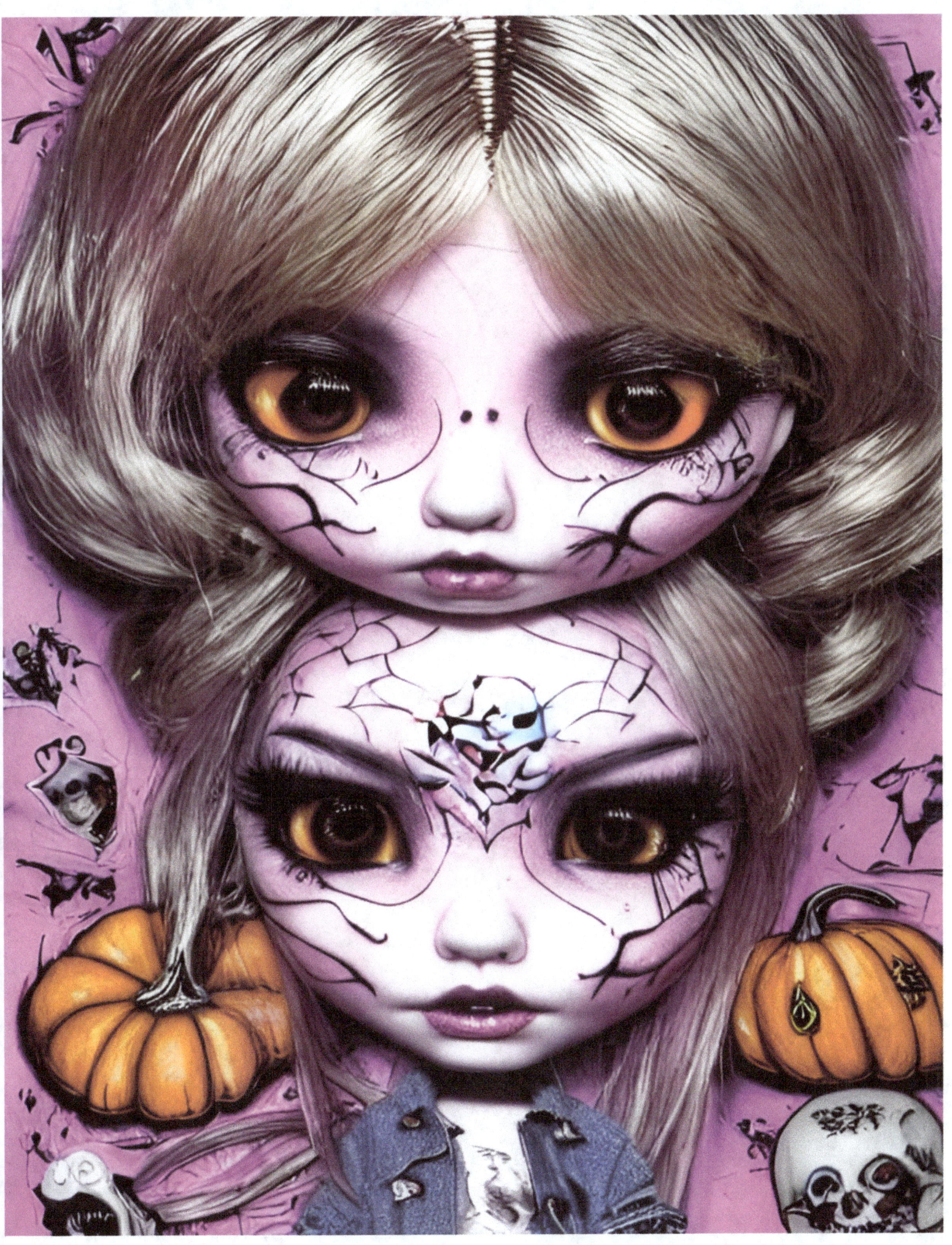

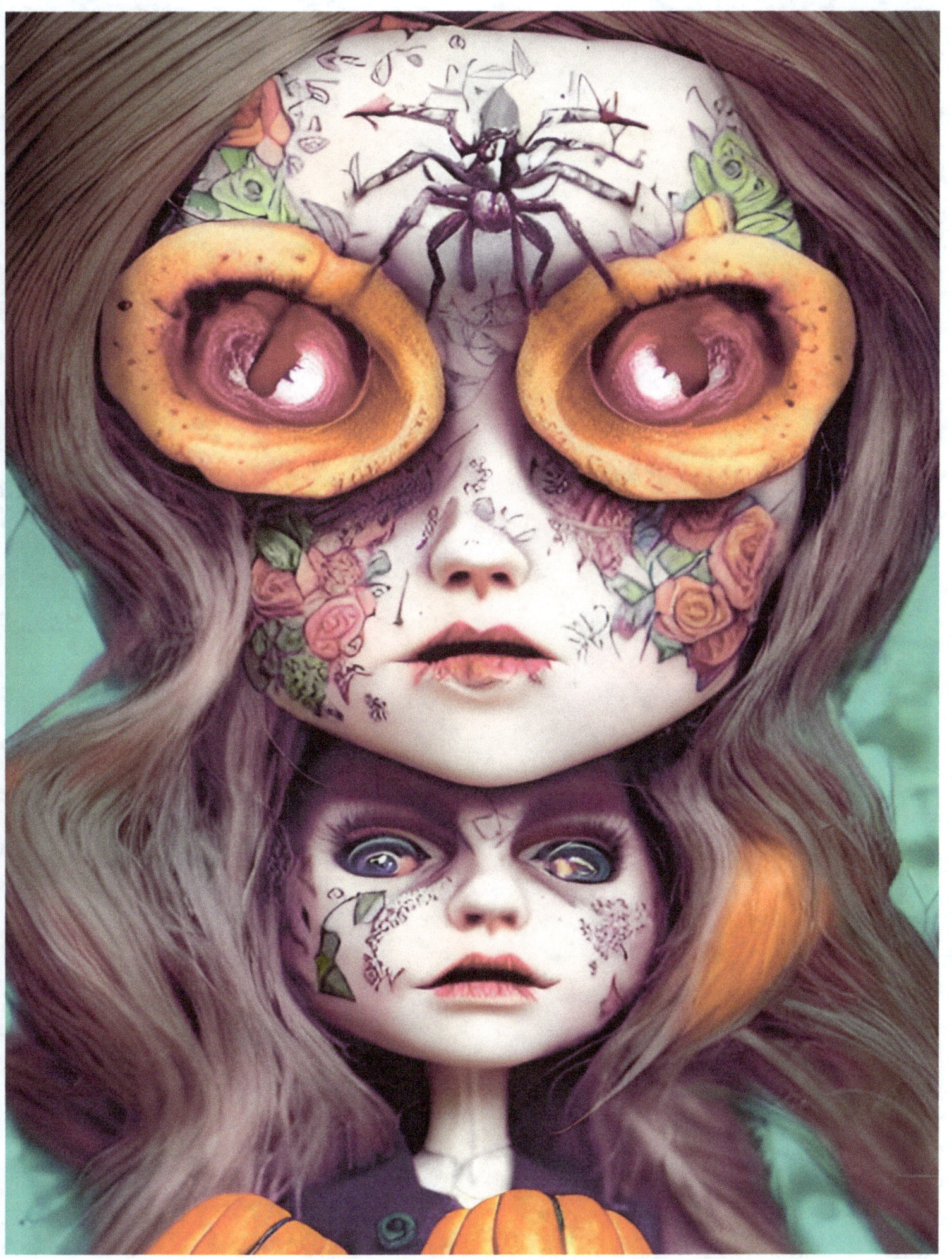

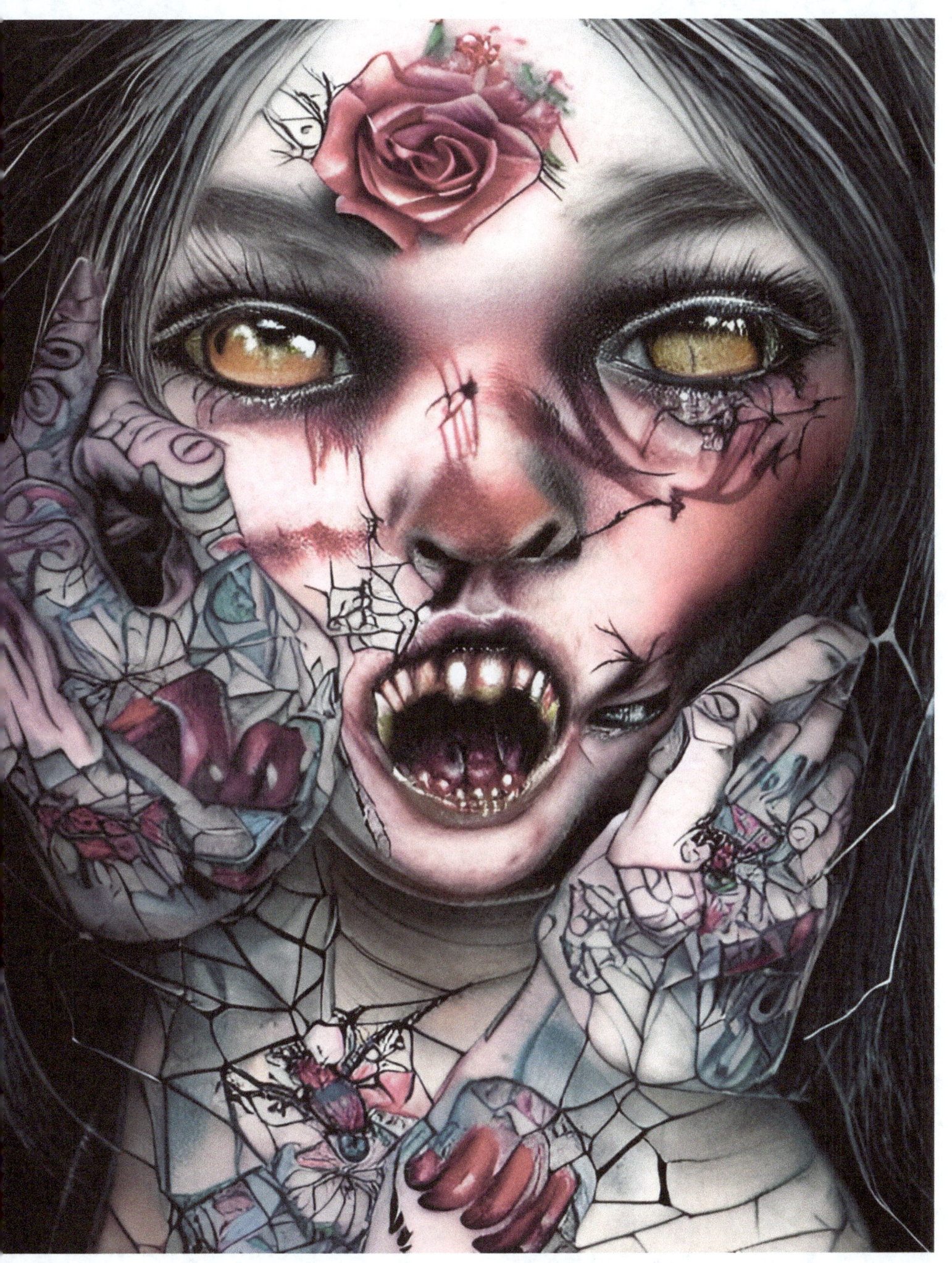

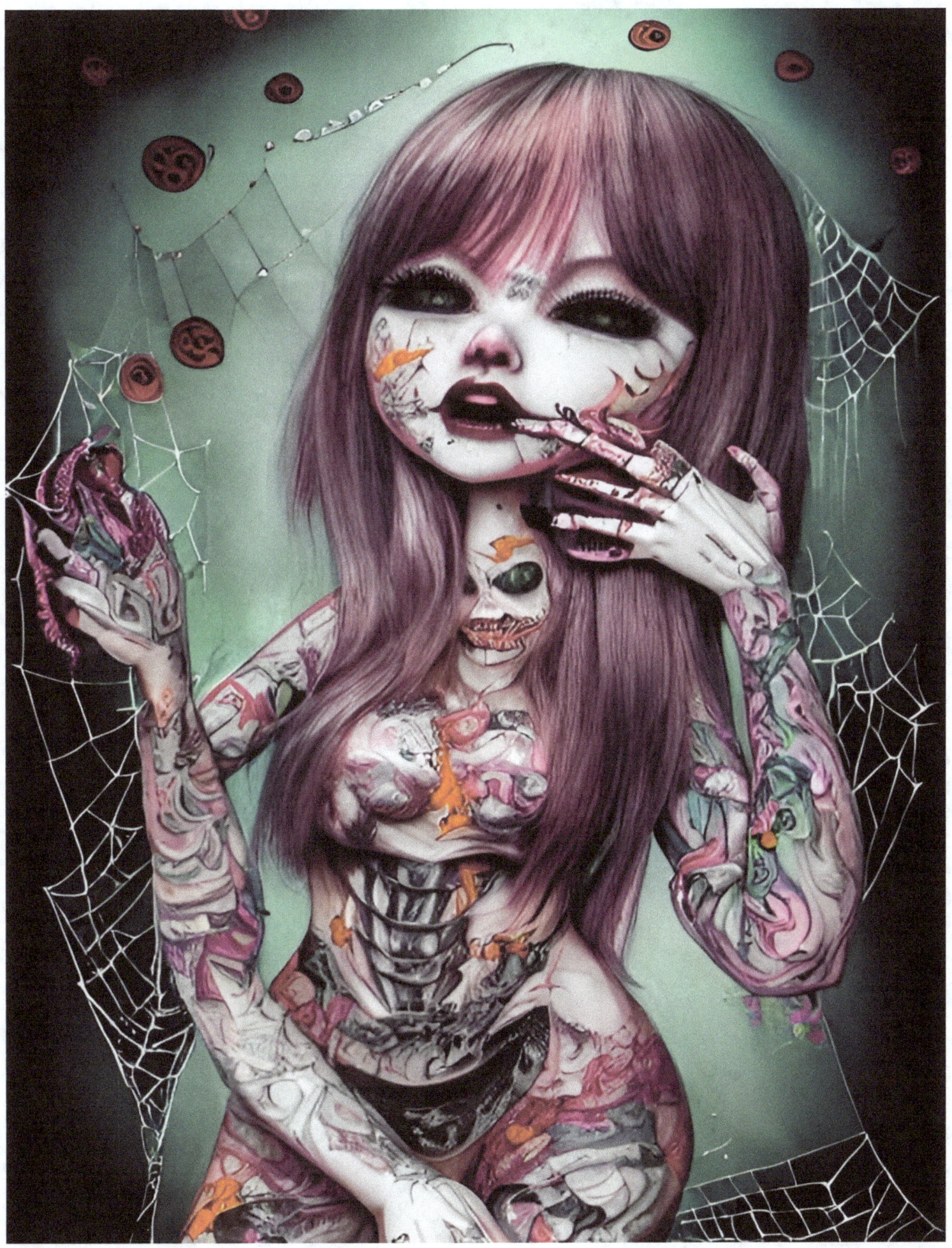

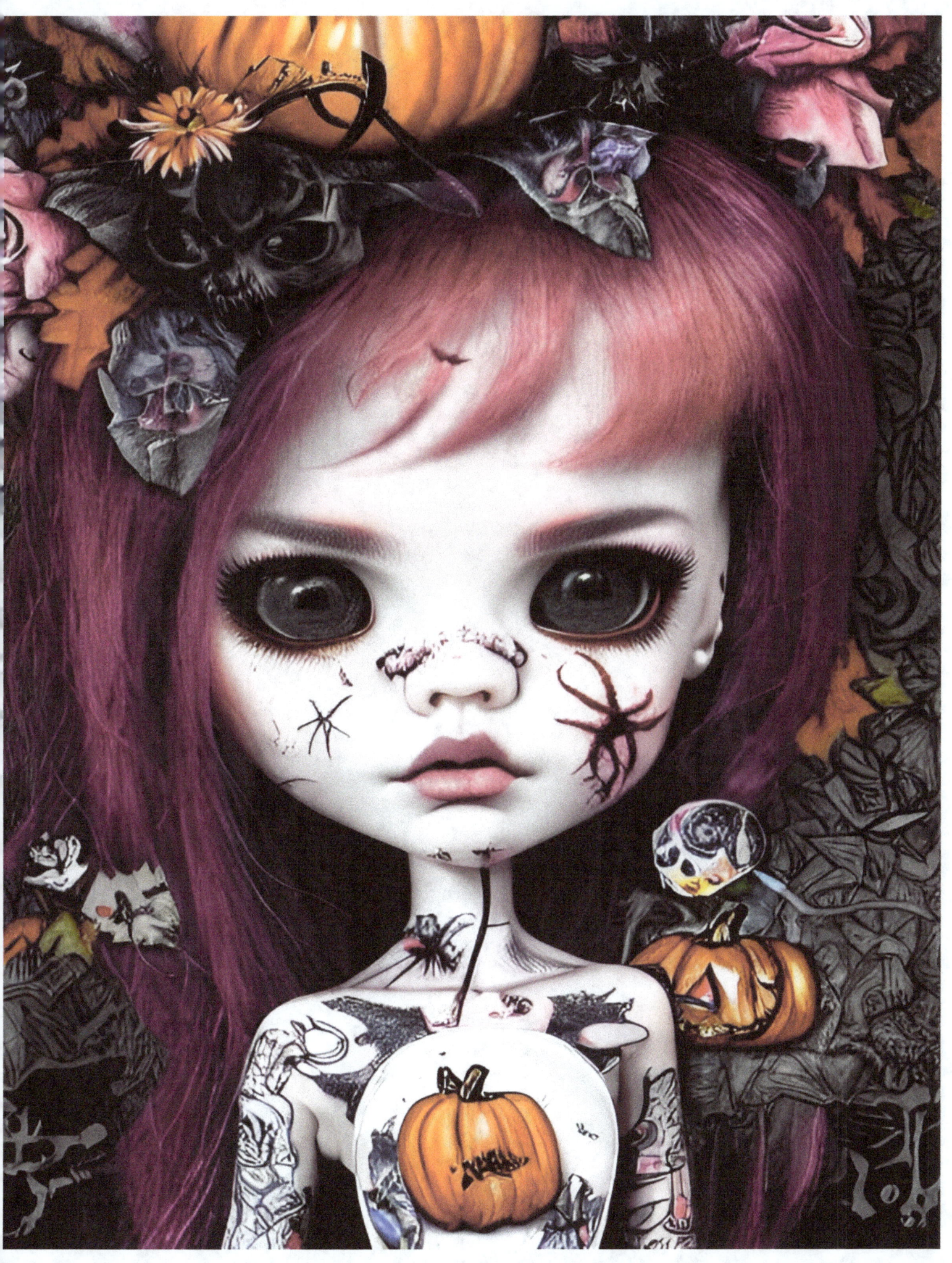